The Observers Series
BUTTERFLIES

About the Book

This is a completely new edition of *Observers Butterflies*, covering every species of British butterfly, with descriptions of their complete life cycle from egg to adult butterfly. It is illustrated in full colour throughout, using the magnificent colour plates of butterflies painted by A. D. A. Russwurm and R. B. Davis from the originals of F. W. Frohawk, and now widely regarded as among the finest butterfly paintings ever produced. Each meticulously drawn plate shows both the top and the underside of the butterfly wing for ease of identification. The totally revised text by Paul Morrison also encourages close observation, with information on each species: their habitat, location and preferred foodplants, revealing the secret personality of every butterfly. Notes on photographic techniques and recording charts are included and the latest conservation measures for British butterflies are discussed.

About the Author

Paul Morrison is a professional wildlife photographer, author and lecturer. He studied at Reading University where he specialized in marine biology, freshwater ecology and entomology. After graduating he taught biology and botany for five years, before leaving to gain commercial experience within the pharmaceutical industry, medical publishing and computer graphics industry. Now living in north Buckinghamshire, he runs his own natural history photographic library, *Natural Selection*, and markets his own photographs and those of other specialist photographers. His photographs have appeared in a variety of wildlife books and magazines and on television programmes. Paul Morrison is an advisory member of the British Botanical Society and British Butterfly Conservation Society and has written numerous magazine articles on butterflies, specializing in their conservation and protection. He has also been guest lecturer on special interest cruises and is a tour leader for several wildlife tour companies.

He is the author of *Bird Habitats of Great Britain and Ireland*, published by Michael Joseph.

The *Observer's* series was launched in 1937 with the publication of *The Observer's Book of Birds*. Today, over fifty years later, paperback *Observers* continue to offer practical, useful information on a wide range of subjects, and with every book regularly revised by experts, the facts are right up-to-date. Students, amateur enthusiasts and professional organisations alike will find the latest *Observers* invaluable.

'Thick and glossy, briskly informative' – *The Guardian*

'If you are a serious spotter of any of the things the series deals with, the books must be indispensable' – *The Times Educational Supplement*

⊙ O B S E R V E R S

BUTTERFLIES

Paul Morrison

Colour plates of adult butterflies by
A. D. A. Russwurm

Colour plates of early stages by
R. B. Davis

Copied from the originals of
F. W. Frohawk

BLOOMSBURY BOOKS
LONDON

With thanks to my mother, who gave me
my own *Observers Butterflies*
nearly thirty years ago and who has provided
constant encouragement ever since,
including typing the manuscript
for this book

PENGUIN BOOKS

Published by the Penguin Group
Penguin Books Ltd, 27 Wrights Lane, London W8 5TZ, England
Penguin Books USA Inc., 375 Hudson Street, New York, New York 10014, USA
Penguin Books Australia Ltd, Ringwood, Victoria, Australia
Penguin Books Canada Ltd, 10 Alcorn Avenue, Toronto, Ontario, Canada M4V 3B2
Penguin Books (NZ) Ltd, 182–190 Wairau Road, Auckland 10, New Zealand

Penguin Books Ltd, Registered Offices: Harmondsworth, Middlesex, England

This edition first published 1989
Illustrations previously published in *Colour Identification Guide to
Butterflies of the British Isles* by T. G. Howarth 1973

This edition published by Bloomsbury Books, an imprint of
The Godfrey Cave Group, 42 Bloomsbury Street, London, WC1B 3QJ,
under licence from Penguin Books Limited, 1992

3 5 7 9 10 8 6

Text copyright © Paul Morrison, 1989
Illustrations copyright © Frederick Warne & Co., 1973

Printed and bound in Great Britain by
BPCC Hazells Ltd
Member of BPCC Ltd

ISBN 1-8547-1018-4

PREFACE

In 1937, when the original *Observer's Book of Butterflies* was published, it was welcomed as the first easily-readable, pocket-sized guide, detailing the various species of the British Isles and describing early life cycle stages too. Between the 1920s and 1940s the summer temperatures were above average, which favoured the breeding habitats of butterflies, so that the author, W. J. Stokoe, was writing in a 'butterfly boom' era. He detailed sixty-nine species of butterfly, covering their identification, habitat and life cycle. The original book also appeared when collecting and 'setting' (or mounting) butterflies were still fashionable, and these practices have been largely replaced today by captive breeding and drawing or photographing live specimens. There can be no doubt, however, that a great deal of our early butterfly knowledge originated from the collectors of the eighteenth and nineteenth centuries.

Since the 1950s summer temperatures have gradually dropped below the seasonal average, and these climatic changes, together with habitat destruction over the last forty-five years as man consumes the countryside for industrial, agricultural and housing needs, have caused the decline of many of our butterfly breeds, and the complete extinction of others. Having been given the opportunity to update completely this legendary book, I have taken the decision to omit certain species covered in the original, either because they were always one-off migrants and are unlikely to be seen again in Britain, or because they have become extinct in the last 130 years. The Long-tailed Blue, for instance, breeds in the Mediterranean and has rarely turned up in Britain, while the Short-tailed Blue, which breeds in southern Europe, was seen in Dorset in 1885 and 1952, but not officially since. The Mazarine Blue used to be a resident species, with colonies last recorded in 1877, and a single sighting in 1908, but is now considered extinct. The Bath White, seen in 1906 and 1945, has not been seen officially since, and the Black-veined White became extinct in 1925, having been a serious pest in the 1860s in the apple orchards of Kent. In 1857, due to over-collecting and the drainage of its natural fenland habitat, our Large Copper became extinct, but I have retained it in this

5

rewritten edition because conservationists have re-introduced a similar Dutch subspecies into Britain, where it is now part of a recolonization scheme. In a similar way the Large Blue became extinct in 1979, but is currently being re-established using a similarly marked strain of the butterfly from Europe, with the aim that it will once again fly across grassy hillsides in southern England. For the first time in *Observers Butterflies*, the Northern Brown Argus is covered fully as a separate species. As recently as twenty-two years ago, many people thought this butterfly was a subspecies of the Brown Argus, and published literature further confused the situation. Today the Northern Brown Argus is recognized as a species in its own right and justifiably has its own place in this book. This edition of *Observers Butterflies* covers sixty-five individual species.

Many butterfly watchers and serious entomologists had their enthusiasm first sparked by the original *Observer's Book of Butterflies*, so I have been careful to preserve its essential characteristics, but at the same time, since we have learnt so much more in recent decades about the behaviour and ecology of butterflies, I have made every effort to include the latest discoveries. Current information shows, for instance, that butterflies have distinct personalities. Some are aggressive, others are shy and retiring, whilst a few are positively gregarious and will actually settle on the observer for a closer look!

I consider myself very honoured to have been asked to provide new text to accompany the beautiful colour plates drawn by A. D. A. Russwurm and R. B. Davis, and seen here for the first time in the *Observers* format, some of which were accurately copied from the classic originals of F. W. Frohawk's *Natural History of British Butterflies* (1924).

The *Observers* series is designed to encourage readers to use their eyes and study things around them. I hope you will be amazed by how much you can learn from accurate, patient observation, but also by how much enjoyment can be had from looking at butterflies flying free in their natural habitat.

PAUL MORRISON

CONTENTS

INTRODUCTION

Butterflies are estimated to have been on this planet for around seventy million years, and yet it is only relatively recently that we have begun to learn anything about them. The aim of this book is to show that they represent a very important part of Britain's wildlife, and are worthy of thorough investigation by anyone interested in natural history. From a world total of 18,000 known butterfly species, only 400 occur in Europe, and of these, 65 can be found in the British Isles. At least nine of these species are rare migrants, and several others are rare or extremely localized in their distribution. The common species, however, include many of the most visually attractive, and the observant butterfly enthusiast can easily see forty species without the need for special expeditions.

Butterfly watching has become very popular in the last fifteen years, with the collector becoming a dying breed and the amateur, but serious, observer increasingly contributing towards butterfly conservation. The number of butterfly farms with walk-in display areas are largely responsible for this increase in butterfly awareness, attracting as many as three million visitors each year. Many of these visitors are awestruck as large tropical butterflies flit close by, and the chance to see some of the smaller, more elusive British species in captivity has also encouraged people to seek them out in the wild. As with birdwatching, 'twitching' (or enthusiastic tracking) has become popular. Keen butterfly watchers visit every habitat within their immediate vicinity, identifying the local species, and then travel further afield throughout the country to record the rarer, localized types, such as the Chequered Skipper, which only occurs in parts of Scotland.

Throughout the species accounts, description of the appearance of each butterfly has been kept to a minimum, because this is so obvious from the detailed illustrations. Instead, space is devoted to the behaviour and ecology of each species, and to the conditions required within the habitat for colonization to occur and for completion of the life cycle. Within the last decade, entomologists (people who study insects professionally) have learnt that it is now not sufficient for the caterpillar foodplant simply to be growing in a particular habitat. Butterflies will ignore the plant if it is not growing in precisely the right conditions of shade or sunlight, for example, and ideal larval conditions are vital for the continued survival and distribution of our butterflies. With sensitively-balanced habitat requirements, butterflies react quickly to any change, and a part of this book therefore looks at man's interference with their habitats and the reasons why butterflies need conserving. Naturally, conservation will only be successful if people increase their knowledge of butterfly behaviour by observing these insects, and this is why another section is devoted to butterfly watching.

Within the next twenty years, a great deal must be done to secure the future of our native butterflies. We need more reserves, with a greater degree of management. More people must be prepared to study butterflies, so that facts about their behaviour and life cycle can be more widely known. There is no need for anyone to undertake these responsibilities on their own, because by joining a society or your county Conservation Trust, you can enjoy butterflies alongside other beginners, and some experts, and eventually become a local expert yourself! There is nothing quite like enjoying your hobby and at the same time making new friends with whom you can exchange notes, observations and even carry out joint projects in the countryside.

BUTTERFLY LIFE CYCLE
AND STRUCTURE

Each butterfly passes through four completely different stages during its lifetime. These stages are, 1 egg or *ovum* (plural, *ova*), 2 caterpillar or *larva* (plural, *larvae*), 3 chrysalis or *pupa* (plural, *pupae*), and 4 butterfly or *imago* (plural, *imagines*). The individual stages are so dissimilar that it is difficult to believe that each stage can lead to the next. Butterflies perform true metamorphosis, whereby a change in both appearance and structure occurs between each stage of development.

Butterfly life begins with an egg, from which emerges a small caterpillar, often with a disproportionately large head. The caterpillar virtually lives to eat, and grows dramatically before changing into a chrysalis. After a period of time, which may be days or months depending on the species, the adult butterfly emerges to fly away, mate and then disperse the species by laying its eggs elsewhere.

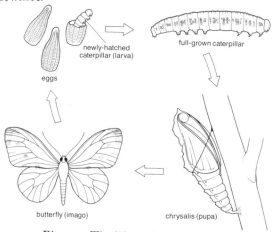

newly-hatched
caterpillar (larva)

full-grown caterpillar

eggs

butterfly (imago)

chrysalis (pupa)

Figure 1: The life cycle of a butterfly

Egg Stage

Butterfly eggs are small and, as can be seen from the species illustrations later in this book, are extremely variable in shape, colour and texture. Some are smooth and glossy, whereas others are ribbed with a dull surface. All eggs have an outer shell, which is sufficiently tough to withstand adverse weather for those species which need to survive winter in the egg stage.

By examining the top of an egg with a powerful hand lens, you will notice a slight depression. This is called the *micropyle*; here the egg shell is thinner and, being permeable, allows moisture and oxygen to pass through to the developing caterpillar. Newly-laid eggs are full of fluid which is slowly absorbed by the microscopic caterpillar embryo, until it grows into a recognizable but minute caterpillar and eventually chews its way out of the egg-shell.

With experience, butterfly species can be identified by their eggs, but initially it is possible to group butterfly species into their families (page 48 ff), according to the shape of their eggs. Butterflies referred to collectively as the 'Browns' lay acorn-shaped eggs, for example, whereas those of the 'Whites' are keeled and bottle-shaped.

Butterflies generally spend a lot of time finding the correct foodplant on which to lay their eggs, although a few exceptions, like the Marbled White, shed them randomly while flying across grassland. The eggs are attached to the larval foodplant by a rapid-drying, glue-like secretion, and may be laid in batches, like the Small

(a)   (b)

Figure 2: Typical egg shape of a) the Browns and b) the Whites

11

Tortoiseshell, or individually, like the Purple Emperor. Most eggs change colour immediately after being laid, and the vast majority never hatch, because they are either eaten by birds and insects or killed by disease. In those eggs which do survive, the caterpillar becomes visible, just before hatching, through the transparent shell.

Caterpillar Stage

Having struggled out of the egg, the small caterpillars of certain species eat the discarded shell before crawling away to hide and feed. Caterpillars are extremely vulnerable to attack from birds, and many others are killed by parasitic wasps and flies, or die from infections caused by bacteria and fungi. Very few caterpillars survive long enough to form a chrysalis and, because they are in constant danger of being eaten, they conceal themselves under leaves, amongst vegetation, or in bark crevices, and often feed at night to avoid detection. With powerful cutting jaws, which move with a sideways action, the caterpillar chews its required leaves, flowers or buds. This is the main feeding stage in the life cycle. The caterpillar's skin is thin and elastic, allowing rapid growth to take place: this is the only stage in the entire life cycle in which actual growth occurs.

The body of the caterpillar is long and consists of a head, followed by thirteen segments. Special small, hair-like cells on the face enable the caterpillar to detect the correct foodplant by 'chemical taste', rather than sight, because its group of six eyes are primitive and virtually useless for visionary detail. They only respond to light intensity, which helps the caterpillar move around the foodplant, since light indicates an upward direction, and dark a downward one. Behind the head are the first three body, or thoracic, segments, which become the *thorax* of the butterfly. Each of these segments bears a pair of jointed, thoracic or 'true' legs, which the caterpillar uses to clasp the foodplant whilst feeding. These true legs correspond to the eventual legs of the butterfly.

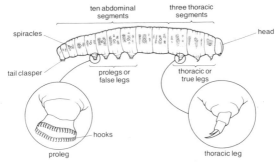

ten abdominal segments — three thoracic segments

spiracles — head

tail clasper — prolegs or false legs — thoracic or true legs

hooks — proleg

thoracic leg

Figure 3: The caterpillar (larva)

Ten abdominal segments form the rest of the caterpillar, and four of them bear pairs of non-jointed prolegs, or 'false' legs. These legs have minute terminal hooks which grip the vegetation and allow the caterpillar to hang on to the undergrowth while moving around from one leaf to another. They are assisted by claspers on the last abdominal segment which hold the caterpillar to a leaf or twig, like a limpet sticking to a rock.

On every body segment except the second, third, twelfth and thirteenth, there are small elliptical holes, called *spiracles*, which allow oxygen from the air to enter the body of the caterpillar, so it can breathe. Some caterpillars are also covered with hairs, spines or warts which are used to help protect them against enemies. These defence structures are often ineffective, however, and most caterpillars have to rely for protection on their coloration and markings which provide camouflage.

Although the skin of the caterpillar is flexible, so much food is eaten that eventually the skin is unable to stretch any further, and it has to be shed. These skin moults are referred to as *ecdysis* and, depending on the species, between three and six full moults occur during the caterpillar's life. Each intermediary stage of caterpillar growth is called an *instar*. As the existing skin reaches its maximum stage of growth, the caterpillar forms a new, larger skin beneath it and, as the old skin splits at the back of the head, the caterpillar emerges by rhythmically pushing the discarded skin towards the tail claspers. Immediately after a moult, butterfly caterpillars have a different colour and sometimes a different shape, but after a few hours (during which the caterpillar often stops feeding and rests) the original appearance returns, though in a larger form. In the final instar, the caterpillar reaches its optimum size and stops feeding altogether. It crawls away to find a suitable place to form the chrysalis. It is usually possible to tell if a caterpillar is about to form its chrysalis because the body contracts and becomes fatter, and the surface colour changes. On this occasion when the caterpillar skin splits for the final time, a perfectly-formed chrysalis emerges.

Chrysalid, or Pupal, Stage

During this part of the life cycle, the cells forming the body of the caterpillar break down and change into cells which make up the adult butterfly. The developing insect does not feed and there is little movement, apart from the occasional abdominal twitch if the pupa is touched. Although it is soft and moist when first formed, a mature pupa is hard because of its special surface material, *chitin*.

Since the pupa is immobile it needs to be perfectly camouflaged for protection and the place where it forms is carefully chosen by the caterpillar. Pupae of some species resemble hanging dead leaves, whereas others formed on the ground are uniformly brown and blend in perfectly with the soil. Pupae of all butterflies are grouped according to three methods of attachment.

1 *Hanging pupae*

When the caterpillar of butterflies like the Small Tortoiseshell or Meadow Brown finds a spot to pupate, it spins a pad of silk on a stem or leaf, and grasps it with its tail claspers. It then hangs free, with the head pointing downwards. Inside the suspended caterpillar the transformation to pupa is taking place, and finally, when the skin splits, the pupa rhythmically wriggles to free itself of the old caterpillar skin. At the tail end this skin is still attached by the claspers to the silk pad. During the process of internal tissue change, the claspers have become a small, hard, tail-like structure called a *cremaster*, which still bears minute hooks similar to those of the claspers and prolegs of the caterpillar. The old caterpillar skin is gripped between the last two tail segments of the pupa and the cremaster is quickly drawn from inside this skin and pressed into the silken pad, where its hooks once again anchor it firmly in position. A series of violent jerks is then performed to dislodge the shrivelled caterpillar skin from the silken pad, so that the pupa alone can hang in position.

2 *Girdled pupae*

The caterpillar of species like the Brimstone and Swallow-tail spins a silken pad like that of the hanging pupa, but it also spins a silk girdle. This surrounds the thorax and supports the pupa with head uppermost. In these species the pupa is firmly attached by both cremaster hooks and silk girdle.

Figure 4. Pupa emerging from caterpillar skin

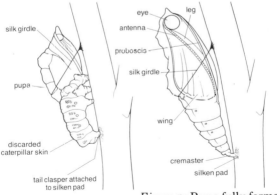

Figure 5: Pupa fully formed

15

Generally it is moths which form a true cocoon around the pupa, but the caterpillars of butterflies such as the Common Blue and Brown Argus spin a loose cocoon, consisting of a few silken threads, around themselves before pupating inside. They may then hang either by cremaster alone or additionally by a girdle. Some pupate completely free of any suspension device and lie deep in root tussocks, or just beneath the soil surface.

Butterfly Stage

Immediately the pupa has been formed, surface features are clearly visible which correspond to parts of the butterfly developing within. At the head end, large swellings occur where the compound eyes of the insect will finally appear, and the wing, antennae and leg outlines are recognizable. The *proboscis* (or tongue), which is coiled in the free-flying butterfly, lies straight and in the centre of the undersurface of the pupa.

When the butterfly is ready to emerge, the pupa darkens considerably. The colour of its wings and all the other features can be seen through the pupal case, which eventually splits behind the head to allow the butterfly its freedom. The butterfly pushes with its legs against the inside of the pupa, whose now brittle walls break open, and the crumpled, fluid-bloated insect crawls free and clings to the pupal case. Emergence is a critical time for the defenceless butterfly. Its wings are small and wrinkled and the first thing the insect will do instinctively is pump blood into the wing veins until they reach full size, when they are held motionless to dry and harden. This process may take up to two hours, during which excess fluid is discharged from the abdomen and the body becomes more streamlined.

While the butterfly is drying its expanded wings it is possible to observe it closely. The large head is dominated by a pair of compound eyes, two sensory antennae used for balance and smelling, and the coiled but extendable

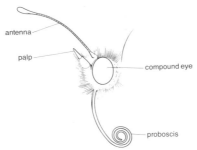

Figure 6: Head of a butterfly

proboscis. The proboscis is used for drinking nectar, juice from rotting fruit in autumn, aphid honeydew, running sap from damaged trees, and various other liquids. When the proboscis is coiled beneath the head, it is protected by a pair of *palps* which form a sheath.

The thorax comprises three segments, each with a pair of jointed legs bearing claws at the end; the second and third segments also each have a pair of wings. In many butterflies, all the legs are of equal length and fully functional, but species of the *Satyridae* and *Nymphalidae* (pages 51–53) appear to have only two pairs of legs because the first pair are very short and useless for supporting the insect.

The wings are formed by an upper and lower thin, transparent membrane, stretched across a network of supporting veins which also supplies them with blood. Miniature scales cover these thin membranes, each one slotting into grooves and overlapping the next slightly to produce a surface similar to a tiled roof. In the course of regular flight and as the butterfly ages, several scales are dislodged and shed as a fine powder, eventually causing the butterfly to look worn and untidy. Some of the scales are pigmented to produce characteristic colours; others are slightly ridged, reflecting or absorbing light and causing the overall colour of the wing to change, depending on the angle from which it is viewed. The iridescent colour

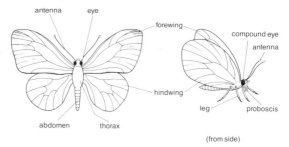

Figure 7 : The Large White butterfly

of the male Purple Emperor and lustrous sheen of the Adonis Blue are produced in this way.

Although the butterfly's wings are primarily for flight, their coloration has other functions. The undersides are generally drabber and help camouflage the resting butterfly, when its wings are characteristically held closed. Males with their brighter colours attract passing females who are persuaded to mate. On the upper forewings, males of certain species show a darkened band of specialized scent scales, which release stimulating odours during courtship and are used to attract the female, rather like human aftershave! Other wing scales produce false eye spots, which deceive attacking predators into believing the vulnerable head is elsewhere. Patches of dark scales on the upper surface also absorb sunlight and warmth when the butterfly is basking.

For the butterfly observer, the colour and pattern of the scales provides a means of identification. They occupy distinct regions of the wing area, although the veins are similarly placed in all species, as shown in Figure 8 opposite.

The abdomen of the butterfly comprises ten segments, but only eight are superficially visible and the other two are modified to form the internal reproductive organs. Female butterflies generally have a rounded, plump abdomen terminating in an egg-laying duct, or *ovipositor*, and males have a thinner abdomen ending in the claspers

18

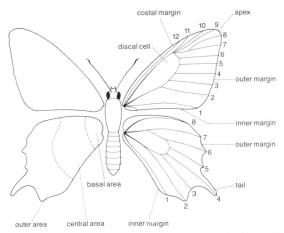

Figure 8: The main veins and wing areas of a butterfly

used to join with the female during mating. Many species enact a fascinating and elaborate courtship before actually mating, when the two butterflies connect at their abdominal tips with heads pointing in opposite directions. Unlike the caterpillar, the butterfly does not grow during its lifetime and exists primarily to mate, with the female laying as many eggs as possible in different areas to distribute the species.

Butterflies all have the potential to live for several weeks and some live for many months, even hibernating through the winter. Most butterflies survive only a few days however, before falling victim to a predator. As each day ends, they roost with wings closed, clinging on to vegetation or upside down under a leaf. The next day butterflies have to bask in the morning sunshine to raise their body temperature to around 33°C so that they can fly. To achieve this, their wings are held wide open, to offer the greatest surface area to absorb the sun's rays.

Moth or Butterfly?

Although they are quite similar in appearance, there are several features to look out for which help distinguish between a moth and a butterfly.

1 Butterflies are daytime flying insects, favouring warm sunlight for basking and feeding activities, whereas the vast majority of moths are nocturnal. In summer, you may often see the Painted Lady butterfly flying just after dusk, but this is the exception; just as a few moths like the Scarlet Tiger and Burnets fly regularly in bright sunshine.

2 At rest, butterflies hold their wings vertically over their backs, like hands held together in prayer, but moths settle in a variety of positions, either with the wings held flat, or draped around the body like a cloak. The Dingy Skipper is the one exception to the rule in British butterflies, because it holds its wings like a moth.

3 The majority of moths have extremely hairy bodies which make them look fatter and larger than they are in reality. Butterflies also possess body hair, but it is generally more streamlined, making their bodies look thin and tapered.

4 Butterfly antennae are always slender and the tip is swollen or clubbed, whereas antennae of moths are extremely variable. Those of the Burnet moths are curved and club-shaped and so closely mimic a butterfly, but all other moths show feathery, frond-like, or strand-shaped antennae. This is the most accurate means of identification of the two insect types.

5 The wings of butterflies are generally brightly coloured, whereas moths, with a few exceptions, have wings in drab shades of yellow, brown or grey.

6 During flight, the fore and hindwings of moths are anchored together by a special hook device called a *frenulum*. Butterflies have no such connection between the wings.

BUTTERFLY HABITATS AND COLONIZATION

The majority of British butterflies breed in closely-knit colonies, which vary in size from less than thirty individuals to several hundred, depending upon weather conditions. Certain sites in Dorset have over 50,000 Adonis Blues, but this size of colony is very unusual and becoming scarcer as habitats dwindle. Other species are more nomadic, dispersing throughout the countryside and breeding and colonizing wherever ideal conditions are found. The Small Tortoiseshell, for example, is found in most counties in the British Isles. In addition, each summer migrants, such as the Red Admiral and Clouded Yellow, arrive from Africa and the Mediterranean in fluctuating numbers.

Although it is impossible to predict accurately where mobile, nomadic butterflies can be observed, it is acceptable to group butterflies according to their favourite habitats, which provide the most suitable breeding conditions and allow discrete colonies to survive.

Woodland

Typical Species – Speckled Wood, Ringlet, Small Pearl-bordered Fritillary, Pearl-bordered Fritillary, Silver-washed Fritillary, Heath Fritillary, Large Tortoiseshell, Comma, Purple Emperor, White Admiral, Duke of Burgundy Fritillary, Brown Hairstreak, Purple Hairstreak, Black Hairstreak, Wood White, Brimstone, Chequered Skipper

Woodland represents the richest butterfly habitat in Britain, and some English deciduous woods have as many as forty species breeding. Further north, where climatic conditions are less tolerable, the number of species declines. The two main types of woodland in Britain are the broad-leaf deciduous and the coniferous. Since tree density determines the survival of butterflies, the deciduous wood is the most productive, with woodland flowers along open rides and glades providing nectar and a source of food for various caterpillars.

Deciduous woodlands used to be managed by coppice rotation, by which undergrowth and some trees were cut back, allowing smaller stands of hazel and hornbeam to grow beneath the dominant oak. Only one part of the wood was coppiced at a time. The following season, with the reduced canopy allowing extra light to penetrate, woodland flowers bloomed in profusion and attracted butterflies. Most species need both sunshine and shade to breed, and unless today's woodlands are managed to prevent rides and glades becoming totally overgrown, the butterflies will gradually disappear.

Because deciduous trees take longer to reach maturity and produce commercial timber than conifers, there has been a huge swing towards conifer plantations in the last few decades. The trees are planted so close together that little sunlight reaches the woodland floor, and any flowers eventually die through lack of light. Few butterflies survive these conditions, but wherever trees are thinned out to create fire breaks and clearings, then butterflies like the Small Heath and Scotch Argus begin to colonize.

Wayside and Hedgerow

Typical Species – Wall Brown, Gatekeeper or Hedge Brown, Green Hairstreak, White-letter Hairstreak, Orange-tip

Hedgerows bordering fields and meadows have been a part of the British countryside for hundreds of years. Although changes in farming methods since 1945 and larger machinery have meant that thousands of miles of hedgerow have been removed, butterflies still fly along those that remain. Spraying the base of hedgerows with weed killers and pesticides has caused the further decline of this habitat, but in rural areas and on the outskirts of towns, where local councils have left the hedgerows and verges unsprayed, the wildflowers and grasses have survived. In such areas, the range of butterflies is encouraging; each spring, when the hazel and sallow catkins are in bloom, Peacocks, Small Tortoiseshells and Brimstones stop to feed. The Green Hairstreak is perfectly camouflaged, sitting on the bright green leaves of hawthorn when the buds first break. The hedgerow has also become the final sanctuary for the White-letter Hairstreak. Ancient hedgerows were interspersed with elm trees where the butterfly laid its eggs, but when Dutch elm disease struck in the early 1970s, most of the trees died, and only sucker growth remains for the caterpillars to live on.

Grassland

Typical Species – Marbled White, Meadow Brown, Small Heath, Dark-green Fritillary, High Brown Fritillary, Small Blue, Brown Argus, Common Blue, Chalkhill Blue, Adonis Blue, Large Blue, Small Copper, Dingy Skipper, Grizzled Skipper, Small Skipper, Essex Skipper, Silver-spotted Skipper, Large Skipper

As a habitat, grassland comes in many different forms, from the chalk downs of southern England to meadows where neutral soil allows tall grasses and flowers to grow together. The short-turfed, south-facing slopes of downland are receptive to butterflies, because a wide range of specialized flowers and grasses grow there. The richest grasslands provide a mixture of short, medium and long grasses, and if successfully managed by grazing, can encourage as many as twenty species of grassland butterfly to breed.

Heath and Upland Moor

Typical Species – Mountain Ringlet, Scotch Argus, Grayling, Large Heath, Silver-studded Blue, Northern Brown Argus

Confined to lowland Britain and in the process of being rapidly destroyed by man, heaths occur wherever ancient woods were felled to reveal sandy soil which was then unable to develop into mature grassland. Heath vegetation is limited and generally includes heather, gorse, bramble and a few grasses which are constantly threatened by fires.

Only the Grayling, which prefers the driest spots, and the localized Silver-studded Blue are characteristic heath-land butterflies. The latter species favours moister areas near long heather, on which it perches during mating. Moorlands tend to replace heaths in upland Britain. They are wetter, due to poor drainage, and the soil is peaty rather than sandy. They form a bleak habitat, frequently on the side of mountains, where the Mountain Ringlet and Large Heath butterflies choose to survive in bogland up to 2,600 feet (800 metres) above sea level.

Freshwater Wetland

Typical Species – Marsh Fritillary, Large Copper, Green-veined White, Swallowtail

Wetland habitat includes marshes, fens and broads as well as rivers, ponds and lakes, but very few butterflies colonize this habitat, and those which do are by no means exclusively confined to it. The Marsh Fritillary can be found on wet meadows and low-lying bogland, but also colonizes dry grassland, where flowers abound. Likewise, the Green-veined White commonly flies around ditches, stream banks, low-lying flood meadows and watercress beds, but can also be found along the shaded margins of woodland.

The Large Copper and Swallowtail are true wetland species and both are magnificent insects. Unfortunately distribution is restricted because their traditional wetland habitats have largely been drained to provide agricultural pasture. Since the Swallowtail is now confined to a few broadland sites, its future is additionally threatened by boating and other water sports, despite being protected by the Wildlife and Countryside Act (page 27).

Coastal Regions

Typical Species – Monarch, Queen of Spain Fritillary, Glanville Fritillary, Painted Lady, Camberwell Beauty, Pale Clouded Yellow, Clouded Yellow, Berger's Clouded Yellow, Lulworth Skipper, Essex Skipper

Very few butterflies actually colonize this harsh, alien habitat and the majority of those listed above are migrants, observed along the coast before flying to other habitats inland. In Britain only three species can be considered coastal: the Lulworth Skipper, confined to the cliffs of Dorset, around Lulworth Cove; the Essex Skipper, which colonizes salt marshes, although it is also found inland on rough grassland; and the Glanville Fritillary, which occurs on the undercliffs of the Isle of Wight and the Channel Islands, barely surviving in colonies carefully managed by entomologists.

Coastal regions are the best places to observe butterfly migration, and since there are many unanswered questions about this phenomenon, it is useful to record all sightings, together with the time of day, weather conditions, and numbers of butterflies seen arriving within a given period (see the Butterfly Record chart on page 36).

Park and Garden

Typical Species – Red Admiral, Small Tortoiseshell, Peacock, Holly Blue, Large White, Small White

The enthusiastic gardener can easily attract butterflies to the garden by planting suitable flowers (see page 44), but only a few species will actually breed in this man-made habitat, because most gardens are maintained by destroying the very plants caterpillars need to survive. The caterpillars of butterflies found in gardens feed on weeds, or cultivated varieties of wild plants growing in fields and hedgerows. The Orange-tip, for example, typically a butterfly of shaded hedgerows, has in recent years moved into suburban gardens, where the eggs are laid on honesty, grown for its decorative seed heads. The Holly Blue is increasingly widespread because the larval foodplants, holly and ivy, are grown in public parks. This fascinating butterfly can regularly be seen within a few miles of the centre of London.

As your knowledge of butterflies increases and your ability to identify species improves, you will doubtless want to know why a certain species colonizes a particular habitat and why it remains there. This type of information is called 'behavioural ecology'. The answers to your questions will come from further butterfly watching and records of your observations kept over a number of years.

BUTTERFLIES AND THE LAW

The most recent, comprehensive step to protect British wild animals and plants was taken on 30 October 1981, when the House of Commons and the House of Lords approved, and therefore made law, the Wildlife and Countryside Act, 1981. As well as protecting our own wildlife, the Act was designed to comply with international agreements; in particular, the Convention on the Conservation of European Wildlife and Natural Habitats, sometimes simply called the Berne Convention. Wildlife experts advised politicians that it was not enough to protect the species alone, because the habitat also requires an organized degree of protection if the species is to survive.

Every five years the Nature Conservancy Council, which is the government body promoting nature conservation in Britain, has an opportunity to review the 1981 Act. During 1986, new recommendations were put forward to the Government for approval. They were based on evidence that some animals and plants had become rarer and were now in greater danger of disappearing than they had been when the Act was passed. In December 1987, the Secretary of State for the Environment accepted these suggestions and they became law, with further recommendations now not possible until 1991.

The Wildlife and Countryside Act, 1981, is divided into different parts, called Schedules, depending on the type of animal or plant and the level of protection. It is Schedule 5 which protects rare insects, including butterflies. Only three species of butterfly are currently listed as specially protected: the Heath Fritillary, Large Blue and Swallowtail used to survive in woodland clearings, short-turf grassland and wetlands. Because of habitat destruction they have either become extinct and re-introduced, or extremely localized to one or two areas in Britain. It is an offence to 'kill, injure, take, possess or sell any of these butterflies, or to damage, destroy or obstruct access to any place they colonize or breed, or to disturb them while they are in the habitat'. Such protection has become necessary for these species to survive in Britain, and although the restrictions may seem severe, they do have their value. In 1981 the Chequered Skipper was also given this protection, following its extinction in England during 1976. The species then became confined to West Scotland, but with protection, its numbers have increased. It is now considered to be out of danger as a breeding insect in Britain, so in 1986 it was removed from the Schedule 5 list. Even so, its long-term future will still depend on habitat availability and sanctuary from over-enthusiastic butterfly collectors. Whereas controlled collecting of common species, which has occurred for several centuries, does little to affect the overall population, greedy and indiscriminate collecting of rare and localized species causes serious damage to their populations. It can be contributory to their decline, as has happened with some Duke of Burgundy colonies in recent years.

It is important that the reader should not see 'Legal Protection' as an overpowering, official restriction to hinder those interested in rare butterflies. The protection is simply necessary for some species to survive longer, and thus allow more people to enjoy them. Conservation itself is a matter of education by which people are encouraged to use their eyes and be aware of the environment around them, and the animals and plants living within a habitat.

BUTTERFLY CONSERVATION

Rural Britain has been completely altered since the end of the Second World War. In the last forty years an area of unspoilt countryside the size of Buckinghamshire, Bedfordshire and Oxfordshire, has been built upon, while open countryside between the expanding towns and cities has also been changed by man. Lowland fens have been drained, 50 per cent of all the ancient deciduous woodlands have been felled and 60 per cent of the unique lowland heaths have disappeared. Each year 4,000 miles of hedgerow are grubbed out to make fields larger and 95 per cent of our rich flower meadows, so valuable as a source of nectar for butterflies, have been lost to the plough. Britain's countryside has suffered as intensive farming, industrialization and urbanization have triumphed and as habitats disappear, so does the local wildlife. Butterflies have particularly suffered, because they require such a delicate balance in their environment. Their numbers fall once pollution or habitat disturbance begins, and they can be viewed as a barometer, immediately indicating the health of the countryside. Although conservationists cannot entirely prevent industrial development, they can campaign to protect and maintain areas of the countryside where butterfly colonies are significant.

Some of the dangers to butterfly species are not immediately obvious. When the Large Blue became extinct in 1979, it was partly because some of the thyme-covered hillsides where it lived were destroyed by ploughing, but a change in the nature of the habitat was also a major factor. The butterfly had always thrived on grassland which had been regularly grazed by sheep or rabbits, because the caterpillar spent part of its life underground in ants' nests (see page 122), and the ants themselves only survive where the turf is short. As grazing became uneconomical, farmers removed their sheep from the hillsides. Also, rabbits died in their thousands because of the fatal disease myxomatosis, which struck Britain in

1953. With both these natural 'lawn-mowers' gone, the wild thyme, which formed part of the larval food cycle, became smothered, as coarse grasses and scrub vegetation took over. Eventually the ant colonies died out, and with them the Large Blue disappeared from Britain.

In recent years, butterfly experts have learnt that conservation requires a knowledge of the insects' life cycle and the natural habitat requirements necessary for each species to breed and survive. Once this information is known, further conservation involves management of the habitat to make sure these important conditions are maintained. Today, many butterflies survive on downlands, flower meadows and in woodlands because conservationists are making sure their habitat conditions remain ideal. The Large Blue has now been re-introduced, from similar European stock, to protected managed sites in the West Country. During the summers of 1986 to 1988 adult butterflies could be seen on the wing, egg-laying. The re-introduction scheme will now attempt to establish colonies on different sites, some with public access.

Fortunately, habitat management for butterfly conservation has become very popular within County Naturalists' Trusts. Because we now know that butterflies remain fairly close to the area where they emerge, all over the country the character of sites is being maintained, so that the butterfly populations will increase. No single habitat should be looked at in isolation, because for a variety of butterflies to survive in one area, an equally varied set of conditions will be necessary. Butterflies need a mosaic of small habitats within an overall larger habitat. The Peacock and Red Admiral feeding on your garden buddleia in late summer are probably there because a small patch of stinging nettles in a neighbour's garden provided food for the caterpillars! (See page 47.) A habitat mosaic is equally necessary on grassy hillsides. For example sheep, fenced and allowed to graze in an organized rotation, provide areas of short turf for butterflies like Adonis Blues and Silver-spotted Skippers, and zones where nectar-supplying plants like knapweed and field scabious grow amongst taller grasses encourage Marbled Whites, Meadow Browns and Large Skippers.

The ancient coppiced woodlands of Britain offered a mixture of mini-habitats with naturally overlapping boundaries. In the open sunny glades, bugle, primroses and violets grew and attracted Pearl-bordered and Silver-washed Fritillaries, while along the woodland ridges, various other plants thrived which encouraged egg-laying Wood Whites and Ringlets. Bordering many of the old woodlands, flowery meadows and hedgerows attracted butterflies towards the edges of the wood, where they became established. Today, any woodland managed as a butterfly reserve needs to provide similar intricate mosaics. Different species use several mini-habitats at different times of the day, with varying requirements as their life cycle progresses throughout the year. Woodland management is extremely complex, and the margins should be maintained as carefully as the interior, since some woodland butterflies, such as the Brown Hairstreak, prefer to bask in the sunshine along the edges of the wood and lay their eggs there too.

Future conservation of butterflies in any habitat will depend on a careful compromise between man's requirements and preservation of the environment. If marshland has to be drained for farming, then some of it should be left undisturbed, so that the birds, insects and flowers which depend on it can remain, even if the farmer has to be financially compensated for leaving valuable land for wildlife. This approach has arrived too late for some species, but is an encouraging sign for the future of others. For years, farmers were expected to maintain maximum production from their land, but this eventually resulted in surpluses of corn, meat, butter and cheese, of benefit to nobody but the producer. The Government finally announced in 1987 that a balance must be set between output and needs. Two million acres of farmland had been taken out of production, so some of it was given back to wildlife. Particularly important stretches of countryside were designated Environmentally Sensitive Areas (ESAs), with the Ministry of Agriculture providing grants to farmers in exchange for an agreement to allow wildlife, including butterflies, to survive on the land. Butterflies will only continue to survive if fertilizers and insecticides are controlled, since many species are killed by sprays applied to destroy pests.

The weather and climate also have a significant effect on butterfly populations, with dry, warm summers producing more adults. When temperatures are low, females are reluctant to lay eggs. The eggs they do lay also take longer to hatch, and the resulting caterpillars and pupae are slower to develop, making them more liable to fall prey to birds.

Butterfly conservation must be viewed in geographical perspective, too. Because Britain is at the northern limit of the natural range of many European species, as climatic conditions change, certain butterflies will subsequently become rarer. This biological contraction of range is happening right across Europe as seasons alter, and consequently butterfly populations arc falling not only because of man's destruction of the habitats but also because of natural climatic changes over which he has no direct control. All conservationists can do for certain species, is to provide sites where declining populations can temporarily survive before their inevitable extinction because of climatic changes.

The inevitability of some of our butterfly species declining cannot be disputed, but we *can* do something about the non-climatic threats to their existence. No butterfly has ever colonized Britain from abroad, so we must conserve those species which already breed here. How dull our summers would be, if our blue butterflies no longer danced across the downlands, and the bright yellow male Brimstone failed to brighten the woodland margin each spring.

OBSERVING BUTTERFLIES

Some of the habitats previously described will be found close to your home, and after regular visits, experience will tell you which are the best sites within each habitat. Areas where flowers grow and which are sheltered, or which receive full sunlight some time during the day, are popular with butterflies. Alternatively the margins of woods, undisturbed roadside verges and disused railway tracks are excellent haunts. Nothing can match the enjoyment of sitting on a chalk downland slope in high summer, observing dozens of different butterflies fluttering over the grass, avidly feeding on wild thyme or marjoram, or basking on bird's-foot-trefoil.

One of the attractions of 'butterfly watching' is the fact that these are daytime flying insects, almost worshipping the sun, so it is pleasurable to be observing them when the weather is at its best. Also, there are so many unanswered questions about butterfly behaviour (such as how often each species feeds and what are the favourite sources of nectar, how vigorously territories are defended, or where the insects roost at sunset) that it is always possible for the keen and organized amateur to make some new scientific discovery.

Such information can only be recorded by watching live butterflies living out their life cycles in the wild. Fortunately, the collectors with their nets and killing jars, which turned interesting insects into lifeless ones, have largely been replaced by patient observers who make notes about, or photograph (page 39), what is actually going on in front of their eyes. It is far more challenging and rewarding to record unpredictable, frequently unknown butterfly behaviour than to look at dead specimens in cabinets, where fresh air is replaced with the smell of mothballs.

Observing butterflies requires as much expertise and practice as birdwatching, so do not get despondent if you are unable to identify positively, or understand the behaviour of, every species you see during your first session. With time, the accuracy and depth of your observations will increase, and your written field observations, recorded over several seasons, could be extremely valuable in increasing our knowledge of butterflies, since personalized accounts of butterfly behaviour are still few and far between.

Much of the behavioural information given in the species accounts in this book is a result of my own fifteen years of butterfly watching, and the importance of structured records cannot be overemphasized. The type of chart I use is reproduced overleaf. It is designed so that for any day all the different species colonizing one habitat can be seen at a glance. Space is provided for details of the time of day sighting occurred, locality, and plants growing in the habitat, together with any behavioural information. The record chart can be reproduced on individual A4 sheets and the season's work filed in ring binders for quick reference. It can, of course, be easily modified for your own requirements.

Some of the information requested might appear to be very obvious, but the date, for example, is vital to help correlate the butterfly flight period in wild conditions, especially as in good seasons, double or treble broods occur. Since the weather varies from year to year, dates taken in isolation are insignificant, but considered together with weather conditions, they enable a flight pattern to emerge from one year to the next.

Sunshine is essential for regular flight, so butterflies are more active in the sun than on cloudy days, when they choose to roost, frequently below flower-heads, and on tall grass stems. The importance of sunlight to butterflies can be seen by watching them flying along a disused railway embankment. When they reach the shadow cast by a bridge or viaduct, they fly up and over the bridge, rather than risk cooling down in its shadow. Persistent winds, especially those coming from the north-east, render many species inactive, as does heavy rainfall, although some butterflies, like the Wall Brown, Ringlet and Dark-green Fritillary, will fly in moderate rain.

The time of day should always be noted, because we need to know more about when butterflies feed or fly. It is already known that in colder periods butterflies become active later in the day, suggesting that air temperature is more critical for activity than specific periods of the daylight hours. The air temperatures also control when the insect emerges from the pupa. The Scotch Argus, for example, confined to mountain boglands of northern Britain, does not emerge until mid-July, when temperatures are higher, and requires at least 22.5°C (72°F) to stimulate courtship or mating. Recording such information over a period of years makes it possible to predict which species should be on the wing at certain temperatures. Equally, as regional temperatures fluctuate annually, an unnecessary trip to a distant site can be prevented by checking your records against local weather reports before departing.

Habitat details and its precise locality, using Ordnance Survey map references, are very useful, especially if you are trying to compare distribution of species in one particular habitat and another similar one nearby. Purple Emperors colonizing one Surrey woodland site detailed with grid references on your records, are also likely to occur in neighbouring woods, wherever the necessary foodplant grows. Butterfly watching is not always predictable, however, and some species may be observed well away from their usual habitat.

Never feel that an observation is not worth recording; you may be one of the few people ever to have seen that behaviour. Some butterflies have a favourite perch, often a twig or flower with a commanding view, which they repeatedly return to. Once you have discovered this, you can sit and allow the butterflies to come to you. If the favourite perch happens to be on a territorial boundary, you may then witness fights between rival males.

Counting butterfly species within a habitat is important to assess local populations and monitor annual fluctuations, especially as these variations may be related to weather conditions during the breeding season, or

BUTTERFLY RECORD SHEET

	1	2	3		1	2
Chequered Skipper				Orange-tip		
Small Skipper				Green Hairstreak		
Essex Skipper				Brown Hairstreak		
Lulworth Skipper				Purple Hairstreak		
Silver-spotted Skipper				White-letter Hairstreak		
Large Skipper				Black Hairstreak		
Dingy Skipper				Large Copper		
Grizzled Skipper				Small Copper	✓	A
Swallow-tail				Small Blue		
Wood White				Silver-studded Blue		
Clouded Yellow				Brown Argus	✓	B
Brimstone	✓	A		Northern Brown Argus		
Large White	✓	C		Common Blue	✓	
Small White	✓	B		Chalkhill Blue		
Green-veined White				Adonis Blue	✓	D

COLUMN INFORMATION

1 Species observed
2 Numbers
3 Courtship/mating or egg-laying

ABUNDANCE OF SPECIES

A = 1 — 6 present
B = 7 — 12
C = 13 — 20
D = 21 — 50
E = abundant

DATE 21/8/82

HABITAT Short-turf downland with some scrub

SITE DETAILS O.S. map 174 Ref 577828 Moulsford Downs, Berks

	1	2	3		1	2	3
ly Blue				Silver-washed Fritillary			
ge Blue				Marsh Fritillary			
ke of Burgundy Fritillary				Glanville Fritillary			
ite Admiral				Heath Fritillary			
rple Emperor				Speckled Wood	✓	A	
d Admiral	✓	A		Wall Brown	✓	C	
inted Lady	✓	A		Small Mountain Ringlet			
all Tortoiseshell	✓	C		Scotch Argus			
rge Tortoiseshell				Marbled White			
acock	✓	A		Grayling			
mma				Gatekeeper			
all Pearl-ordered Fritillary				Meadow Brown	✓	A	
arl-bordered tillary				Small Heath	✓	C	
gh Brown Fritillary				Large Heath			
rk Green Fritillary				Ringlet			

ATHER SUMMARY Warm sunny spells, with occasional oud cover. Light south-westerly breeze, but no signs rain. Air temperature appeared constant.

IE OF DAY 2 – 4 pm.

DITIONAL NOTES/PHOTOGRAPHIC DETAILS Turf well-grazed by sheep nd rabbits with bare soil patches where Adonis Blues asked. Flowers included horseshoe vetch, self-heal, ellow bedstraw, wild thyme and field scabious

HER SPECIES OR RARE MIGRANTS SEEN

After K.J. Willmott

disturbance of the habitat. Whatever the cause, population records make it possible to foresee a species decline and conservationists can act to improve habitat conditions before it is too late.

Watching the courtship of a pair of butterflies prior to mating is one of the rarest sights, since it only happens on a few days each year for each species. By using a set of historical records and with good planning, the chances of observing courtship are improved. Normally, males emerge from the pupa first and, wherever necessary, establish the territory which they will occupy until death, allowing only females to enter. Male butterflies always need to chase their partners, often with rapid aerial twists and dives, until their advances are accepted. For courtship to be successful, the females must be previously un-mated. In some species, the amorous males drum on the back of the females' wings with their antennae, making audible clicks. Each species probably has a finely-developed courtship ritual, but many of these are unknown. Such secrets are waiting to be discovered, as are the precise times of day when the mated females actually lay their eggs.

There are many aspects you can investigate in your area, which have never been studied before, all just requiring careful observation. How do butterflies protect themselves? What are the main predators of each species? What time of day do butterflies stop flying during perfect weather?

At the end of the day on a warm, south-facing grassland slope, butterflies can be seen going to roost if you kneel and examine the grass and flower-heads at eye level. Elsewhere, Brimstones begin to roost in bramble patches as early as 3 p.m., even during high summer. They find a secluded perch, hidden from predators and protected from rain, where they fold their wings and disappear from view. These facts have only been learnt from butterfly enthusiasts who have spent time watching. There is still far more to discover from patient observation in city or suburb, wood or moor, where butterfly life still remains something of a mystery.

38

PHOTOGRAPHING BUTTERFLIES

No matter how keen your eyesight, or how accurate your note-taking, you will not always be able to recall everything you observe on a butterfly-watching trip. Information from a recent weekend observation is not too difficult to remember, but details of a trip several years ago are impossible to keep in your mind. For this reason, photography has become extremely popular as a practical method of recording butterfly species, their characteristics, life cycles and habitats. Whether colour-print or transparency film is used, photographs, fully labelled, dated and collated, can be used for reference for many years. Photographing butterflies is a natural development from observing them in the wild.

Photographs will only be useful as records if the butterfly is clearly and sharply captured on film, and since most species have a wingspan of two inches (five centimetres) or less, the camera and lens used for butterfly photography must be capable of focusing on relatively small insects at close range. The final choice of camera and accessories will be determined by cost, but since butterfly photography nearly always involves carefully stalking the insect and holding the camera by hand, without the use of a tripod, the best type of camera is a single lens reflex (SLR) which can take a variety of lenses, including a close-up or macro lens. These cameras are relatively lightweight, with the distinct advantage that whatever you see through the viewfinder will appear on the resulting photograph.

Obtaining good photographs of butterflies in the wild takes practice, and a certain amount of luck, and you must also accept that the task is very time-consuming. They are easily distracted, nervous insects, and any rapid movement will cause them to fly away, as will your shadow, if you allow it to fall across the butterfly. Therefore, apart from luck, success will also require patience and perseverance, together with some behavioural knowledge of the insects.

Eventually, as you become more successful, you will set

39

your own standards for a good photograph. Generally photographing butterflies from the side, when their wings are closed, or from above, with wings open as they bask requires the camera being held parallel to the insect before firing the shutter. In this way, sharp images, clearly identifying the species, can be collected. If you want to be a little more ambitious, a head-on view can be attempted whilst the proboscis is probing into a flower for nectar. With this type of photograph, it is impossible to get all of the butterfly absolutely sharp, but it is important to make sure that the head, antennae and forward wing edges are in focus.

To obtain attractive butterfly photographs, four main rules should be followed:

1 Get close enough to the subject to achieve an identifiable picture of it, with some indication of the natural habitat.

2 Make sure the butterfly is not moving, which will cause a blurred photograph.

3 Use adequate light to illuminate the butterfly.

4 Make full use of the depth of field (see below).

Acceptable photographs of butterflies or any other natural history subject depends on the camera aperture used, and this rather awesome term 'depth of field'. It is important therefore to understand these terms before trying to take a successful photograph.

Aperture

The iris diaphragm of a lens controls the amount of light reaching the film. The lens is calibrated in numerical apertures (f-stops) which change in increments: f.1.4, f.2, f.2.8, f.4 . . . f.16, f.22, etc.

Depth of Field

When a lens at full aperture, i.e. f.1.4, f.2, f.2.8, is focused on a subject at a specific distance from the camera, only the subject is in sharp focus. But as the diameter of the lens opening (aperture) is reduced, areas in front of and behind the subject become more clearly defined and 'acceptably sharp' – though not as sharp as the main subject. The region that extends from the point of acceptable sharpness nearest the camera to a similar point that is farthest from the camera, is termed depth of field.

Depth of field increases as the lens aperture is reduced, – f.16 giving greater depth of field than f.4. It also becomes greater as the camera-to-subject distance is increased. The region of acceptable sharpness in front of the subject is half that of the region of acceptable sharpness behind it.

Getting close to butterflies depends on the weather conditions and your approach. Stalking the insects should be practised regularly, so that you become expert at quietly and slowly creeping towards them in a straight line. When you get within camera-firing distance, remember to move the camera and your hands slowly towards your eyes, because jerky movements will disturb your quarry. The most gentle of breezes can frustrate your efforts, because a butterfly resting on a flower-head will constantly sway in and out of focus. A still, sunny day is the best time to practise stalking butterflies. On cloudy days, and first thing each morning, butterflies are inactive and rest on vegetation, but although they will be easier to photograph, they will be more difficult to find, and their wings will be closed, revealing only the duller undersides to the camera.

Single lens reflex cameras have variable shutter speed facilities, which you can make use of to stop subject movement, by setting the speed to at least 1/125th of a second. However, since shutter speed has to be linked with lens aperture to get the correct exposure, the depth of field at fast shutter speeds declines, along with the degree of sharpness.

Electronic flash will help provide sharp, well-defined photographs, since the duration of the flash light is so short that it acts as a stroboscope and freezes any movement of the insect or camera shake. Using this artificial light at close distances means that smaller apertures can be used,

to get maximum depth of field, with well-illuminated subjects. However, dark shadows can occur behind the butterfly, because a single flash gun mounted on the camera fires directly at the insect, throwing an unattractive shadow on to the background. Two small flashguns, one slightly less powerful than the other, mounted on a bracket either side of the camera, overcome this shadow problem. With a special pistol-grip mechanism, obtainable from a camera shop, the whole apparatus can be hand-held during stalking (see opposite). Most cameras have a flash synchronization speed of 1/60th or 1/125th of a second, so once the camera is set up to fire the flash guns the process of stalking the resting butterfly can begin. The ideal shooting distance with a 50 mm or 100 mm macro lens is about 15 inches/38 centimetres and with the flash arrangement described, will allow apertures of f.11, f.16, or f.22.

Correct exposure when using flash for close-ups will have to be determined by a trial run of exposures. It is well worth using up a fair amount of film in order to find the positioning of the flashguns for correct exposure at pre-selected apertures and working distances, since the distance from the flashguns to the butterfly is important. If you always keep notes of apertures used, film speed and brand, flash-to-subject distance and even the lens used, these can be referred to in future situations. Precise details of flash techniques are beyond the scope of this book, but further information can be found in titles appearing in the 'Recommended Books' list on page 190.

The best place to practise butterfly-photography techniques is in your back garden, especially around buddleia (page 45), where numerous species feed on the nectar for up to fifteen minutes, allowing ideal opportunities for critical focusing and capturing several shots during each session. Butterfly photography presents a challenge which cannot be expected to be mastered overnight, but as with all new hobbies, patience will eventually pay off, the technique will become second nature, and inspiring photographs of butterflies will be yours for the taking.

BUTTERFLIES IN THE GARDEN

Some butterflies are entirely dependent on one habitat. The Silver-spotted Skipper, for example, depends completely on chalk grassland, where the turf is short and the caterpillar foodplant, sheep's fescue grass, grows. No species of butterfly is similarly dependent on the garden as a habitat. Since butterflies are mobile however, many can be attracted to visit gardens if flowers are provided as a source of nectar.

Over the last century the countryside has changed, and destruction of habitats in the last forty-five years has escalated to disastrous levels. Wetlands, old hay meadows, chalk downlands, heathlands and deciduous woodland have disappeared throughout Britain because of urban expansion, and industrial and agricultural development (see page 29, 'Butterfly Conservation'). In many parts of Britain, butterfly decline has occurred because wild flowers have become scarce and have been replaced by miles of barren cereal fields. Since by instinct butterflies emerging from a pupa fly away to disperse their species, they frequently disperse into a biological desert.

Perhaps never before have back gardens been so important as wildlife oases and, since butterfly habitats are declining elsewhere, the sixteen million gardens throughout Britain represent a valuable potential habitat for these attractive insects. Eighty per cent of the population of Britain has access to a garden, and is thereby responsible for a small part of undeveloped land which can be controlled. Any careful and environmentally concerned gardener can attract butterflies to visit and feed on a rich and varied supply of nectar. The rarer species of butterflies are unlikely to visit gardens, but those that do include some of the most colourful. Unfortunately, wherever cabbages and nasturtiums are grown, two pest species will also follow – the Small and Large Whites, often referred to as the 'Cabbage White' butterflies.

Gardens can become sterile places for butterflies if the owner regularly attacks the plot with weed killers, herbicides and pesticides, or hoe, rake and lawn mower, because, although a perfectly manicured garden results, butterflies prefer a more disorganized, wild environment. Planting beds of nectar-bearing flowers, in sites where they receive full sunlight and protection from the wind, will draw butterflies into the garden, and make them reluctant to leave. If an additional area is created which is suitable for breeding, then the whole life cycle of certain species can be enacted in the garden. The breeding area will require some regular management and, since butterflies only lay their eggs on specific larval foodplants, a certain amount of botanical and butterfly knowledge (all to be found within the pages of this book) will also be required.

One of the most familiar butterfly attractants is the buddleia, which becomes smothered in insects from July to September, when the pale mauve flowers are in bloom. The bush always responds well to a hard pruning in spring. However, a wide range of annuals, perennials and shrubs will draw butterflies, and by careful planning it is possible to create a flower border which is not only attractive to these insects, but visually pleasing to humans too, with a succession of blooms from spring until autumn. Sallow willow, with its soft, downy catkins, blooms in March and April and provides an early source of nectar for the spring butterflies. Later, sweet rocket and honesty attract Orange-tips and Green-veined Whites. The peak of the butterfly season is June and July, when thyme, sweet-william, marjoram, red valerian, lavender and the shrub hebe act as successive nectar traps for butterflies. As autumn approaches, sedum or ice plant and michaelmas daisies provide a valuable source of food, and Red Admirals, Small Tortoiseshell and occasionally the Comma will feed on fermenting plums and apples left rotting on the ground.

A typical butterfly border can be laid out as shown overleaf. You must be prepared for the plants to take a few seasons to mature however, and remember, if the summer weather is bad, fewer butterflies will survive to visit the border anyway.

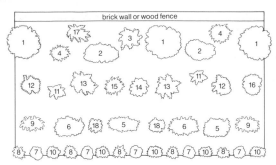

Figure 9 : A typical butterfly border

KEY

1 Buddleia	7 Aubretia	13 Tobacco plant
2 Sweet rocket	8 Bugle	14 Honesty
3 Hebe	9 *Primula denticulata*	15 Lavender
4 Michaelmas daisy	10 Yellow alyssum	16 Buckthorn
5 Sweet-william	11 Sedum (ice plant)	17 Sallow willow
6 Red valerian	12 Marjoram	18 Thyme

To provide a butterfly-breeding nursery, a gardener must maintain an area free of all sprays, where wild grasses, thistles and nettles can grow. Since both short and tall grasses are required by different species, a habitat mosaic, with patches of short and long grass growing alongside each other, should be created by cutting one area regularly, and leaving another uncut. Unfortunately, rye grass, which is sown for the majority of lawns, is not eaten by any British butterfly caterpillar. Grass mosaics therefore need to be planted with short-growing red and sheep's fescue, common bent grass or annual meadow grass, and tall, coarser grasses, including cocksfoot, meadow foxtail and wood false brome. Some of these species can become invasive so the 'butterfly gardener' will need to keep them controlled, but the bonus will be colonies of Gatekeeper, Meadow Brown and possibly Ringlet.

46

The grass mosaic will provide larval foodplants, but adult butterflies need to be attracted by planting some wild flowers and, where the grass only grows up to five centimetres high, clover, thyme and bird's-foot trefoil can be sown. The latter plant also provides egg-laying sites for the Common Blue and Dingy Skipper. Knapweeds and field scabious are suitable flowers for planting amongst the taller grasses. Wild flowers and appropriate butterfly grasses are now widely obtainable from nurseries and seed merchants (some of which are listed on page 189), and once established, sow their own seeds to help create larger patches. The low-growing wild flowers are not harmed by light mowing and the flowers will bloom again between mowing cycles.

Small patches of stinging nettles are necessary to attract breeding Small Tortoiseshell, Peacock, Comma and Red Admiral butterflies. They must be grown in a sunny, sheltered position, or they will be ignored by the butterflies. If they are cut in spring and summer, young succulent leaves form which the butterflies favour for egg-laying. In spring, when the Brimstones awake from hibernation, they enjoy feeding on the nectar of aubretia, polyanthus and yellow alyssum, but the caterpillars feed exclusively on common and alder buckthorn. If a solitary specimen of one of these shrubs is planted in the garden, it is nearly always found by egg-laying females. In a similar way, Holly Blues have now become a regular garden or park species because of the availability of holly and ivy for the caterpillars.

Creating a good butterfly garden requires knowledge of the butterflies and their larval foodplant, as well as growing nectar-supplying flowers. As your knowledge improves from watching butterflies in the back garden, careful management of the plot should cause a welcomed increase in butterfly populations immediately on your doorstep, which may disperse into the countryside nearby.

BUTTERFLY FAMILIES
WITH LARVAL FOODPLANTS

There are sixty-five species of butterfly recorded in Britain, including the migrants, and they can be grouped into eight different families. Only sixty species are known to breed in Britain.

1 *Hesperiidae* – The Skippers

All members of this family are small and moth-like with very hairy bodies and short, stumpy wings. There are eight species and all have a rapid, darting flight just above grass height. The majority have golden-brown wings, but two types are grey with white markings.

Name	On the wing	Larval foodplants
Chequered Skipper *(Carterocephalus palaemon)*	May – June	Wood false brome, purple moor-grass
Small Skipper *(Thymelicus sylvestris)*	July – mid-August	Yorkshire fog-grass, wood false brome, cat's-tail grass
Essex Skipper *(Thymelicus lineola)*	July – August	Cock's-foot, creeping soft-grass
Lulworth Skipper *(Thymelicus acteon)*	July – mid-August	Tor grass, chalk false brome, couch grass, cat's-tail grass
Silver-spotted Skipper *(Hesperia comma)*	Late July – early September	Sheep's fescue
Large Skipper *(Ochlodes venata)*	June – August	Cock's-foot grass, wood false brome
Dingy Skipper *(Erynnis tages)*	May – June, late August	Bird's-foot-trefoil, horseshoe vetch
Grizzled Skipper *(Pyrgus malvae)*	May – June, August	Creeping cinquefoil, wild strawberry

2 *Papilionidae* – The Swallowtails

There are several hundred species of this family, mostly found in the tropics. There are eleven species in Europe but only one, the English Swallowtail, is found in Britain. The large butterfly, with yellow and black wings with long tails, is unmistakable.

Name	On the wing	Larval foodplants
Swallowtail (*Papilio machaon*)	Mid-May – June, August – September	Milk parsley, wild angelica, fennel

3 *Pieridae* – The Whites and Sulphurs

Members of this family are all medium-to-large butterflies with white or yellow wings. Black markings occur on the majority and a few species have green or orange patches.

Name	On the wing	Larval foodplants
Wood White (*Leptidea sinapis*)	May – June, late July – mid-August	Meadow vetchling, bitter vetch, tufted vetch
Pale Clouded Yellow (*Colias hyale*)	May – September	Clover, lucerne, bird's-foot-trefoil
Clouded Yellow (*Colias croceus*)	May – September	Clover, bird's-foot-trefoil, lucerne
Berger's Clouded Yellow (*Colias australis*)	June – September	Horseshoe vetch
Brimstone (*Gonepteryx rhamni*)	February – October	Common and alder buckthorn
Large White (*Pieris brassicae*)	May – September	Cabbage and other brassicae, nasturtium, mignonette
Small White (*Pieris rapae*)	March – mid-May, mid-June – August	Cabbage and other brassicae, nasturtium, mignonette
Green-veined White (*Pieris napi*)	April – September	Charlock, garlic mustard, hedge mustard, cuckoo flower

Name	On the wing	Larval foodplants
Orange-tip *(Anthocharis cardamines)*	May – June	Garlic mustard, hedge mustard, charlock, honesty, cuckoo flower

4 *Lycaenidae* – The Hairstreaks, Coppers and Blues

All members of this family are small butterflies. The Blues and the Small Copper prefer open grassland, whereas the Hairstreaks are elusive woodland butterflies. The Green Hairstreak is the only Hairstreak without characteristic tails.

Name	On the wing	Larval foodplants
Green Hairstreak *(Callophrys rubi)*	May – June	Rock-rose, bird's-foot-trefoil, dyer's greenweed, buckthorn, dogwood, bilberry, gorse
Brown Hairstreak *(Thecla betulae)*	August – September	Blackthorn
Purple Hairstreak *(Quercusia quercus)*	July – September	Common oak
White-letter Hairstreak *(Strymonidia w-album)*	July – August	Common elm, wych elm
Black Hairstreak *(Strymonidia pruni)*	Late June – July	Blackthorn
Large Copper *(Lycaena dispar batavus)*	July	Great water-dock
Small Copper *(Lycaena phlaeas)*	April – October	Common sorrel, sheep's sorrel, dock
Small Blue *(Cupido minimus)*	Mid-May – June	Kidney vetch
Silver-studded Blue *(Plebejus argus)*	July – late August	Gorse, heather, bird's-foot-trefoil
Brown Argus *(Aricia agestis)*	May – September	Rock-rose, common storksbill

Name	On the wing	Larval foodplants
Northern Brown Argus *(Aricia artaxerxes)*	Late June – July	Rock-rose, common storksbill
Common Blue *(Polyommatus icarus)*	Mid-May – June, August – September	Bird's-foot-trefoil, restharrow, black medick, clover
Chalkhill Blue *(Lysandra coridon)*	July – August	Horseshoe vetch
Adonis Blue *(Lysandra bellargus)*	Late May – June, August – September	Horseshoe vetch
Holly Blue *(Celastrina argiolus)*	April – May, July – August	Spring generation eat holly, autumn generation eat ivy buds
Large Blue *(Maculinea arion)*	July	Wild thyme, later *myrmica* ant larvae

5 *Nemeobiidae* – The Metalmarks

This family of butterflies occurs chiefly in South America and is typically very colourful. In Britain and Europe the family is represented by a single small-sized species, the Duke of Burgundy Fritillary. The markings of this species resemble the true fritillaries of the *Nymphalidae*.

Name	On the wing	Larval foodplants
Duke of Burgundy Fritillary *(Hamearis lucina)*	Mid-May – June	Primrose, cowslip

6 *Nymphalidae* – The Fritillaries, Admirals and Vanessids

Butterflies of this family are medium-to-large in size and generally are powerful fliers. Fritillaries all show either a bright orange or golden brown upper wing-surface, marked with black veins or spots. Other members of *Nymphalidae* have drab underwings, to match dead leaves, but brightly coloured upper wing-surfaces, some with red and orange markings.

Name	On the wing	Larval foodplants
White Admiral *(Ladoga camilla)*	July – August	Honeysuckle
Purple Emperor *(Apatura iris)*	July – August	Goat willow, grey willow
Red Admiral *(Vanessa atalanta)*	May – October	Stinging nettle, hop
Painted Lady *(Cynthia cardui)*	Mid-May – June, August – September	Thistle, mallow, stinging nettle
Small Tortoiseshell *(Aglais urticae)*	March – October	Stinging nettle
Large Tortoiseshell *(Nymphalis polychloros)*	March – October	Common and wych elm, sallow, cherry, aspen, pear, poplar, whitebeam, birch
Peacock *(Inachis io)*	March – October	Stinging nettle
Camberwell Beauty *(Nymphalis antiopa)*	Late August – September	Willow, birch
Comma *(Polygonia c-album)*	March – October	Stinging nettle, hop, elm
Small Pearl-bordered Fritillary *(Boloria selene)*	June – mid-July	Dog violet, marsh violet
Pearl-bordered Fritillary *(Boloria euphrosyne)*	May – mid-June	Dog violet, marsh violet
Queen of Spain Fritillary *(Argynnis lathonia)*	May – September	Sweet violet, dog violet
High Brown Fritillary *(Argynnis adippe)*	Late June – early August	Sweet violet, dog violet
Dark-green Fritillary *(Argynnis aglaja)*	July – August	Hairy violet, dog violet, marsh violet
Silver-washed Fritillary *(Argynnis paphia)*	July – August	Dog violet
Marsh Fritillary *(Eurodryas aurinia)*	Late May – June	Devil's-bit scabious

Name	On the wing	Larval foodplants
Glanville Fritillary *(Melitaea cinxia)*	June – early July	Ribwort plantain, buck's-horn plantain
Heath Fritillary *(Mellicta athalia)*	Late June – July	Common cow-wheat, ribwort plantain, foxglove, germander speedwell

7 *Satyridae* – The Browns

Except for the Marbled White, which is black-and-white, all British members of this family are a shade of brown. They are small-to-medium in size and exhibit an obvious black eyespot on both sides of the forewings near the margin. Other eyespots, frequently with white centres, are characteristic of the hindwings. No species is considered rare, and they live in colonies, flying lazily above tall grasses.

Name	On the wing	Larval foodplants
Speckled Wood *(Pararge aegeria)*	March – October	Annual meadow-grass, cock's-foot grass, wood false brome
Wall Brown *(Lasiommata megera)*	May – mid-June, August – early September	Tor grass, wavy-hair grass, wood false brome, cock's-foot grass
Mountain Ringlet *(Erebia epiphron)*	Mid-June – July	Mat grass
Scotch Argus *(Erebia aethiops)*	July – August	Purple or blue moor-grass
Marbled White *(Melanargia galathea)*	July – August	Red fescue, timothy, sheep's fescue, cock's-foot grass, tor grass
Grayling *(Hipparchia semele)*	July – September	Marram grass, sheep's fescue, bristle-bent grass, tufted-hair grass

Name	On the wing	Larval foodplants
Gatekeeper, or Hedge Brown *(Pyronia tithonus)*	July – September	Cock's-foot grass, annual meadow-grass, couch grass, red fescue
Meadow Brown *(Maniola jurtina)*	Mid-June – late September	Smooth meadow-grass, cock's-foot grass, tor grass, slender false brome
Small Heath *(Coenonympha pamphilus)*	May – September	Annual meadow-grass, woodland meadow-grass, meadow fescue
Large Heath *(Coenonympha tullia)*	Mid-June – July	White-beaked sedge, cotton grass, purple moor-grass
Ringlet *(Aphantopus hyperantus)*	Mid-June – August	Cock's-foot grass, annual meadow-grass, wood false brome

8 *Danaidae* – The Monarchs

Typically these are tropical insects but the Monarch or Milkweed butterfly is famous in North America for its mass migrations covering vast distances.

Name	On the wing	Larval foodplants
Monarch, or Milkweed *(Danaus plexippus)*	July – September	Milkweeds (not found in Britain)

BUTTERFLY DESCRIPTIONS

Notes

Except where indicated, the illustrations of the butterflies are reproduced life-size, with the upper wing-surface on the left and underside on the right. Wherever appropriate, both male ($\male$) and female ($\female$) have been illustrated to show their differences. Wing spans given in the text are average measurements for both sexes.

The illustrations of the eggs are all greatly enlarged, but the other stages of the life cycle are life-size reproductions.

A status abbreviation has been used for each species to help the reader see at a glance whether the butterfly is a regular inhabitant or a visitor. The status is indicated by a letter: R – resident, SM – summer migrant and RM – rare migrant (those species readers can expect to see perhaps once in a lifetime).

Other information given at the beginning of each entry describes the species' typical habitat, where the butterfly usually colonizes, and the time of year it actually flies. Readers can therefore easily see if they are in the right place at the right time when identifying, or looking for, a particular butterfly. However care should be exercised in positive identification, because species can show regional variations, producing separate races or sub-species. Geographical variation is well known in the Large Heath, for example, as explained on page 180. To the uninitiated this can be very confusing, since the markings are so variable that many butterflies will not match illustrations of the usual varieties shown in this book.

CHEQUERED SKIPPER
Carterocephalus palaemon

Wingspan: 29 mm (♂), 31 mm (♀) **Status:** R

Typical habitat: Scrubland hillsides and slopes, bordering small woods

On the wing: May – June in a single brood

Adult: Both sexes of this butterfly are similar, with blackish-brown upper wing-surfaces, clearly chequered with yellow-orange spots which are paler in the female. The undersides are a paler version of the upper surfaces, with a greeny-yellow tinge. The antennae bear black clubs, with orange tips.

Life cycle: The eggs are squat, rounded and white, and are individually laid during June on the blades of purple moor-grass or wood false brome, though they are difficult to find. Hatching inside ten days, the small caterpillars are greenish-yellow with a black collar in the early stages, but by the time full size is reached after the fourth moult, they are green and marked with white lines. Eventually, in their final instar, the body colour changes to buff-yellow just before hibernation occurs. While feeding, the developing caterpillar lives in a tube formed by drawing the edges of a grass blade together with silk. By October it will have formed a silken hibernating chamber, spun amongst the grass, where it will remain until the following March. The buff pupa is formed in April and mimics a piece of dead grass. It hatches within six weeks.

Observation and behaviour: This butterfly lives in small discrete colonies, easily overlooked because the adults are only active in sunny weather, when they fly rapidly across the scrubland slopes bordering rivers and lochs. Using bracken, grasses and bog myrtle as perches, the Chequered Skipper enjoys basking with wings outspread. It can also be approached while feeding from flowers such as bugle. During rain showers or cloudy weather, the butterfly roosts deep inside grass tussocks. Males, being territorial, perch on shrubs and wait for unmated females to pass. Females prefer to lay their eggs on foodplants growing close to oak, hazel and birch scrub, or in small tussocks partially sheltered by bog myrtle.

Distribution: This species was first officially recorded from Bedfordshire in 1798, and was locally common throughout the Midlands until the end of the last century. During this century the Chequered Skipper has seriously declined throughout its range and in 1976 became the first species for over fifty years to be declared extinct in England. Extinction was caused by habitat destruction and changes in woodland management so that woods became too overgrown for the species to survive. The butterfly can still be found in Scotland, where it was first discovered in 1942, near Fort William, Inverness, and where it colonizes damp grassland bordered by birch and hazel scrub.

SMALL SKIPPER
Thymelicus sylvestris

Wingspan: 30 mm (♂ and ♀)   **Status:** R

Typical habitat: Rough grassland, woodland rides, verges and hedgerows

On the wing: July – mid-August in a single brood

Adult: Males (*illustrated*) show a distinct band of black scent scales across the upper surface of the orange-brown forewings, but in all other markings the sexes are similar. Black borders surround the wing margins on the upper surfaces, and wing veins are noticeably black. The undersides are a paler orange-brown, with undersides of the hindwings in particular showing an olive-green tinge. In Skippers the antennae colouring is diagnostic and those of the Small Skipper are black on the upper surface and orange on the lower surface, with red-brown clubs. The similarly-marked Essex Skipper often shares the same habitat, so close observation when the butterfly is at rest is recommended.

Life cycle: Laid in small batches from three to ten, the buff eggs are deposited inside a grass stem sheath, and can only be found by thorough searching, or by watching the female in the process of laying. Yorkshire fog is the most popular larval foodplant, but creeping soft-grass and wood false brome are also used. After three weeks the eggs hatch, and spinning a dense silk cocoon inside the grass stem sheath, the capterpillars hibernate without feeding until the following April. On emerging they form single tubes by pulling the edges of one grass blade together, and here they feed, building new tubes as they grow. When fully grown, the green caterpillars rest on the grass blades and are relatively easy to find by close inspection. The green pupa with characteristic pink beak is found at the base of the foodplant, contained in a cocoon of loose silk and grass blades. The adult hatches within three weeks.

Observation and behaviour: Like many of the Skippers, the flight of the Small Skipper is rapid and darting. The discrete colonies can easily be overlooked, because adults enjoy perching and basking in tall grasses and vegetation. When basking, the typical Skipper stance is adopted, with the hindwings held flat but the forewings cocked half-open. The butterflies like to bask at sunset, just before roosting begins, in the long grasses or beneath the flower heads of knapweeds. Once air temperatures reach around 16°C, the adults can fly and are regularly seen feeding on nectar from thistles, knapweeds, marjoram, field scabious and common ragwort. When a female is egg-laying, she carefully selects mature grass plants by buzzing around the stems before alighting. Moving her abdomen around the stems, she then pushes it inside the leaf sheath and deposits the eggs. Grassland butterflies colonize various lengths of grasses. The Small Skipper prefers long grasses with some shelter.

Distribution: Common throughout most of Britain, this butterfly does not occur in north-east England, parts of Cheshire and Lancashire, north Wales, Scotland or Ireland. Curiously none of the grass-feeding Skippers breed in Ireland although their foodplants often grow there. In England it occurs on grassland as far north as Yorkshire.

ESSEX SKIPPER
Thymelicus lineola

Wingspan: 27 mm (♂), 30 mm (♀)   **Status:** R

Typical habitat: Lightly grazed grassland, woodland margins and rides, and coastal marshes

On the wing: July – August in a single brood

Adult: It was only in 1889 that this Skipper was distinguished from the similar Small Skipper and became known as a separate species of British butterfly. Both sexes are virtually identical, having orange-brown upper wing-surfaces with black borders. The male scent scale markings across the forewing uppersides are little more than black lines. On the undersides the ground colour is pale orange-brown with an olive-green tinge. Impossible to distinguish from the Small Skipper in flight, only close examination when at rest reveals subtle differences between the two. In the Essex Skipper, the antennae are black beneath the terminal clubs and not red-brown, as in the Small Skipper. Also the scent scales in the male of the Essex Skipper are much less conspicuous.

Life cycle: Laid inside the sheath of cock's-foot grass, creeping soft-grass, timothy and wood false brome, the smooth white eggs are deposited between July and August.

Unlike those of the Small Skipper, these eggs overwinter and do not hatch until the following March. As the caterpillars feed and grow, they become greener. After the fourth moult, when full size is reached, the green body is marked with darker green and white stripes. Like those of the Lulworth and Small Skipper, the young caterpillar lives inside a tube formed by binding the edges of a grass blade together with silken threads. When fully grown, it rests and feeds on the open grass blades both during the day and night. Low down in grass tussocks, a coarse silken tent is spun between the blades, and here the yellow-green pupa forms. It is difficult to find, and it hatches inside three weeks.

Observation and behaviour: Because of its close similarity to the Small Skipper, the discrete colonies of this species are often mistaken or overlooked. Essex Skippers prefer drier, patchy soils with bare ground and only a moderately tall turf. Here they like to feed from flowers, preferring self heal, small scabious, creeping thistle, trefoils and knapweeds. Adults enjoy basking right into the evening, and often roost in groups on the seed heads of plantains or grass stems. The complete range of the coarse grasses used as foodplants is still not fully known, but the low level, darting flight of the egg-laying females frequently terminates at one of the species mentioned in the 'Life cycle' section above, although tor grass is used in certain habitats.

Distribution: At one time, the species was thought to be restricted to eastern England, but it is now known to be widespread in southern England, south of the Wash. Isolated colonies exist in Cornwall, Devon and Dorset, and the butterfly will probably be discovered to be more common in these counties as lepidopterists take more time to distinguish its colonies from those of the Small Skipper. Large groups breed on saltmarshes in Sussex, Kent and East Anglia, with equally healthy populations on grassland in Surrey and on Salisbury Plain.

LULWORTH SKIPPER
Thymelicus acteon

Wingspan: 25 mm (♂), 27 mm (♀)　　　　　　**Status:** R

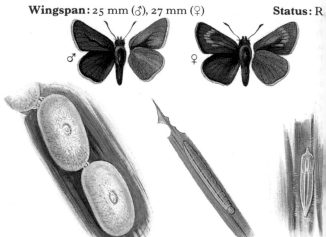

Typical habitat: South-facing hillsides, clifftops and undercliffs

On the wing: July – August in a single brood

Adult: Since this is the smallest of all our golden Skippers and the wings are also darker than other species, it is not too difficult to identify. The upper wing-surfaces of the male are olive-brown with black margins and a patch of scent scales on the forewings, whereas the undersides are yellow-brown. Females are paler, with a circular pattern of gold flecks on the forewing uppersides.

Life cycle: The oval, yellow eggs are laid in small groups of up to six, inside the sheaths of tor grass. Sometimes, even dead stems of the grass are used and the eggs are easy to find in late summer. After three weeks the caterpillar hatches, and without making any effort to feed, hibernates in a small, white silken cocoon formed inside the sheath. The following April, it emerges and grows through a series of moults. It lives in a typical 'Skipper-like' grass-blade tube, emerging at twilight to chew the grass blade immediately above and below its body, thus creating identifiable V-shaped notches. After the fourth moult it is fully grown and its body is light green with dark-green and cream stripes. The caterpillar now dispenses with the tube and rests and feeds on the open leaves. The pupa, which is greenish-white with pink tinges around the head, is difficult to find, deep among the grasses in a loose cocoon. It hatches within a fortnight.

Observation and behaviour: Between eighty and ninety colonies exist in Dorset and some are very large, comprising many thousands of adults. The colonies are discrete and the butterfly is largely sedentary, rarely moving far from the warm grassland slope or undercliff. It seems to prefer ungrazed or partially grazed grass growing to about fifteen centimetres; females prefer the taller clumps of tor grass for depositing their eggs. Like other Skippers, both adults are only active in sunshine and when the air is particularly still, though they are not as aerial as other similar species. Bird's-foot-trefoil is a favourite source of nectar on clifftop habitats, whereas they will feed on marjoram, creeping thistle and ragworts elsewhere. Roosting occurs on tall grass stems in sheltered hollows.

Distribution: British colonies represent the northern limit of the Lulworth Skipper's European range, the majority of British sites being in south-east Dorset. The real stronghold is around the Isle of Purbeck, west to Weymouth. On the military land near Lulworth where this butterfly was first discovered in 1832, up to a million adults emerge in favourable summers. It is most likely that the species is more abundant now than at any other time. Other populations thrive in south-east Devon and Cornwall, near Polperro, but nowhere else. Because the undercliffs it prefers are unstable and therefore unexplored, and the military land has escaped agricultural development, the traditional breeding grounds of this Skipper have been left alone, to its benefit.

SILVER-SPOTTED SKIPPER
Hesperia comma

Wingspan: 30 mm (♂), 36 mm (♀)   **Status:** R

Typical habitat: Heavily grazed downland or old chalk quarries with patches of bare ground

On the wing: Late July – early September in a single brood

Adult: An obvious black bar of scent scales in the middle of the male's forewings helps to distinguish the two sexes. The upper surfaces of the wings are olive brown with golden-yellow spots, which are brighter in the female. The undersides are highly characteristic: both pairs of wings are olive-green, obviously marked with silver spots.

Life cycle: The large, whitish eggs are laid singly on sheep's fescue grass, the only larval foodplant. The eggs will overwinter, and they are easily found attached to the side of the grass blades as autumn approaches. The following March the eggs hatch; the olive-green grub-like caterpillar is difficult to find, living solitarily in a silken tent spun around several grass blades. Towards mid-July the olive-brown pupa is formed, low in the grass stems. It is particularly difficult to find because it is surrounded by a tough cocoon covered with pieces of chewed grass, which provide excellent camouflage.

Observation and behaviour: Few chalkland sites are warm enough to support colonies of this localized Skipper, which is at the northern limit of its European range in Britain. Neither sex will fly unless the sun is shining and temperatures of at least 18°C are necessary to observe the rapid, buzzing flight. Both sexes like to bask on the ground during sunny weather and feed avidly from field scabious, felwort, hawkbit, stemless thistle and carline thistle. They are best observed in this activity with wings held partially open. At night, they roost high in birch trees, beneath dead flower heads or even on scrubland vegetation. Ideal conditions for this butterfly (i.e. bare, worn patches of ground) are only maintained with heavy grazing by sheep or rabbits. Egg-bearing females only begin to lay when the sun shines, selecting small grass tussocks with over fifty per cent of their margins exposed to bare soil. Even if the habitat is heavily grazed, the foodplant growing in thick turf is ignored in preference to that growing near exposed soil, along tracks, near molehills or by rabbit scrapes. Each year the males emerge from the pupae first. They just about tolerate each other, competing for the prize of unmated females. Both courtship and mating take place at ground level and once mated, the females crawl around in the vegetation to prevent approach from other males.

Distribution: This species lives in discrete colonies on warm, south-facing grasslands and, although common in Europe, it is rare in Britain. Within the last forty years, as arable cultivation has increased and rabbit and sheep grazing have decreased, numbers of the Silver-spotted Skipper have drastically declined. Colonies are now confined to calcareous grassland in Hampshire, south Sussex, the southern Chilterns, north Dorset and the North Downs, with additional sites existing in southern Kent. Many of the fifty small colonies in Britain are declining, and only those found on Nature Reserves or specially maintained sites have a guaranteed future.

LARGE SKIPPER
Ochlodes venata

Wingspan: 33 mm (♂), 35 mm (♀)

Status: R

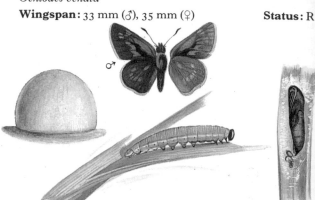

Typical habitat: Tall grassland, hedgerows, road verges, scrubland and its margins and glades

On the wing: June – August in a single brood

Adult: The male (*illustrated*) is identified by a conspicuous black patch of scent scales across the forewings. The upper wing-surfaces are brown, with brighter orange patches towards the body and orange-brown spots elsewhere. These spots are more distinct in the female, but in other respects both sexes are similar. The undersides are a paler orange-brown with a green tinge and the orange dots are fainter. The antennae are long, with clubbed tips, and are back and orange.

Life cycle: The pale-yellow, rounded eggs are laid singly on the underside of cock's-foot grass, wood false brome and occasionally, tor grass. They are difficult to find and hatch within twenty-two days. The small larva immediately pulls a leaf blade together with silken threads, forming a tube in which it lives, feeding externally on the grass blades during the day and night. After the fourth moult, grass blades are bound together with silk and the caterpillars hibernate from September until the following March. When fully grown, they are bluish-green with a darker green dorsal stripe and a cream line running through the spiracles. The dark, almost black, pupa is formed in a loose silken cocoon, made by binding several grass blades together. It can be found by patient searching at the base of grass tussocks in early June. It hatches within three weeks.

Observation and behaviour: Sunny, sheltered localities are favoured by this species, and large colonies may frequently be found. Colonies of Large Skipper, Small Skipper and Essex Skipper sometimes overlap. All three species may fly together, requiring patient observation to distinguish each type of butterfly. The Large Skipper is often overlooked because it enjoys roosting, especially on bramble bushes, but during sunshine and warm hazy weather above 15°C its rapid flight can be seen just above the grassheads. Males are territorial, establishing favourite perching spots on leaves and branches bathed in sunshine, where they wait for passing females. Frequent investigative flights are made and eventually courtship occurs on scrub vegetation about four metres from the ground. Both sexes touch each other with their antennae and the female often leads the male to a mating platform, usually a large, flat leaf. If there are no trees in the habitat, mating takes place in the tall grass. The female then disperses some distance to begin egg-laying. Large Skippers do not feed regularly from flowers, but can be best observed on bird's-foot-trefoil, tufted vetch, fragrant orchid, bramble and thistles.

Distribution: With agricultural expansion leading to the destruction of some of the grassland habitats, there has been some population loss. Generally, however, the Large Skipper is a common butterfly throughout lowland England and Wales. Apart from Dumfries and Galloway, the Skipper is rare in Scotland and is not found on any high ground in Cumbria or on the Pennines. It is totally absent from Ireland.

DINGY SKIPPER

Erynnis tages

Wingspan: 29 mm (♂ and ♀) **Status:** R

Typical habitat: Downland, rough grassland, dunes, heaths and woodland rides

On the wing: May – June or late August, when a second brood is possible in good years

Adult: With grey-brown wings resembling those of a moth, both sexes are alike, apart from a specialized scent-scale pocket on the forewings of the male. All the wings have grey fringes, flecked with brown, and although the intensity of the upper surface-markings varies, the adults always appear drab – hence the English name. The underwings are golden-brown, marked with occasional white spots.

Life cycle: Laid singly on the upper leaf surfaces of birds'-foot-trefoil and horseshoe vetch, the keeled eggs turn orange within a few days and are easy to find. Hatching within fifteen days, the small larva spins a few leaves together and hides in them during the daytime. It is a nocturnal feeder and difficult to find. It reaches full size after the fourth moult, when it is green with a purple-black head. During August, the caterpillar spins a silken *hibernaculum*, or hibernating tent, where it spends the winter, resuming feeding in the spring. In May the dark-green and brown pupa forms inside the hibernaculum and hatches within four weeks.

Observation and behaviour: This frequently-over-looked butterfly forms discrete colonies. The adults enjoy basking on bare ground with their wings held flat to absorb maximum warmth. The males are aggressive by nature but form small groups on the lower slopes of hillsides or in sheltered hollows. Although both sexes visit flowers, females do so more often, choosing birds-foot-trefoil, hawkweeds, milkweeds and buttercups. When they roost, they always do so on dead flower-heads, especially knapweeds, perching with their wings wrapped around their body like a cloak. This moth-like resting position suggests that Skippers are the evolutionary link between the primitive moths and butterflies. They are almost impossible to see when roosting because of their camouflage. Courtship and mating take place deep in the grasses, nearly always on calm days. When the females disperse to lay their eggs, they fly rapidly and low across the turf, selecting foodplants partly covered by other vegetation.

Distribution: This is the only Skipper found in Ireland; a subspecies lives around the Burren in County Clare, which has attractive dark-brown and grey upper surfaces and is far from drab. It is also to be found in Scotland, further north than the Chequered Skipper, but always localized in certain territories. Coastal colonies exist throughout England and Wales, but inland populations are most frequently to be found on downs and in woodlands in the southern counties. North of the Cotswolds and Chilterns, the Dingy Skipper becomes rarer and never occurs on really high ground. Despite being considered a widespread species, it is nowhere near as wide-ranging as the Common Blue, and never as common in the south as the Large or Small Skipper are in their respective sites. Agricultural and forestry developments within the last forty years are responsible for some decline in population throughout its range.

GRIZZLED SKIPPER
Pyrgus malvae

Wingspan: 27 mm (♂ and ♀) **Status:** R

Typical habitat: Downland, rough grassland, woodland glades, sheltered meadows and dry heaths

On the wing: May – June and August, when a second brood occurs during favourable summers

Adult: Apart from the female having a shorter, squatter body, and the male bearing scent scales on the forewings, the sexes are similar. The characteristic chequerboard markings of the upper wing-surfaces cannot be mistaken, and the black-and-white markings are matched by the wing fringes. The undersides are similarly marked, but paler, and the hindwings bear larger, white patches on a greeny-brown background. The antennae are barred black and white, tipped with orange.

Life cycle: Soon after the pale-green ribbed egg is laid, it fades to white and with careful examination can be found on either surface of the leaves of wild strawberry, creeping cinquefoil, bramble or agrimony. After ten days the yellow caterpillars emerge and rest along the midrib on the upper surface of the leaf, where they also feed. Eventually they spin a conspicuous silken tent on the upper leaf surface in which they live, emerging to feed at night. After the fourth moult they reach full size, and are green with dark-brown stripes and a black head. At this stage of their lives they will have spun several leaves together to form a feeding tent, and after two months they begin to pupate. The red-brown pupa shows distinctive white wing-cases and is formed in a loose cocoon at the base of the foodplant, where it overwinters to hatch in May.

Observation and behaviour: Rarely more than a hundred adults form any of the discrete colonies of this butterfly. They are always found in sheltered spots, partly shaded by brambles or scrub vegetation and frequently where the ground cover is thin and there are patches of bare soil for the butterflies to bask on. When the wings are wide open during basking, or occasionally feeding from buttercups, the best views of this small, active butterfly are obtained. In flight they are almost impossible to follow, because swift movements and wing coloration cause their bodies to blur into the background. However, females can be seen purposefully buzzing around the foodplant before laying their eggs and males can be watched vigorously defending their territories. Both plantains and grasses provide favourite roosting perches and last year's dead flower-heads and stems are nearly always selected as the sun goes down.

Distribution: Although in recent years this species has declined because the countryside is being cleared and maintained for agriculture, the Grizzled Skipper is still widespread. Its inconspicuous appearance often causes it to be missed, but colonies can be found in many southern and central counties of England, becoming rarer in the South-west, and north of the Chilterns or Cotswolds. The northern limit of the Grizzled Skipper's range is Yorkshire, where it is very localized, and it is rare in Wales, where it occasionally colonizes clifftops. The butterfly is now extinct in Scotland and absent from Ireland.

SWALLOWTAIL
Papilio machaon

Wingspan: 80 mm (♂), 90 mm (♀)   **Status:** R

Typical habitat: Fens and wetlands in the Norfolk Broads

On the wing: Mid-May – June, with a partial second brood in August – September

Adult: Both sexes of this butterfly are similar, with a pale-yellow ground colour marked with black veins and patches. The hindwings show pale blue borders with orange eyespots and distinctive tails. The undersides have a dusting of yellow across the black markings.

Life cycle: The British subspecies of the Swallowtail is highly sedentary and is restricted to milk parsley as its main larval foodplant. When first laid the individual eggs are yellow, but become brown with age. They are found high on the upper forked leaves of reeds. The small caterpillar hatches within a week, and its black-and-white body, resembling a bird dropping, offers excellent camouflage and protection. After the fourth moult it becomes yellowy-green, marked with black and orange bands on each segment. An extendable orange horn, situated behind the head, gives off a strong odour upon disturbance. After a month the caterpillar pupates, attached by tail hooks and silken thread to form a typical girdled pupa. The pupa is either pale brown marked with black or plain greenish-yellow, both varieties well-concealed on reed or milk parsley stems. In good summers some pupae hatch, producing a partial late summer brood, but the majority overwinter, frequently submerged as water levels rise.

Observation and behaviour: In Europe, the paler continental strain is found flying across dry grassland slopes and flower-rich meadows, but in Britain, the Swallowtail is a fen and reedbed colonizer, requiring large areas of undisturbed wetland. During summer this beautiful butterfly may be seen flying powerfully and gliding down to drink nectar from ragged robin, its favourite nectar source. Its wings continue to quiver even whilst feeding from flowers.

Distribution: Because of the Swallowtail's restricted distribution, it is one of the few butterflies protected by law. Even though reserves are being managed for its survival, however, populations continue to decline and now the Norfolk Broadlands are the last stronghold.

WOOD WHITE
Leptidea sinapis

Wingspan: 42 mm (♂ and ♀)   **Status:** R

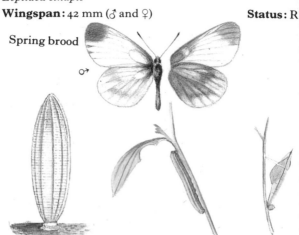

Spring brood

♂

Typical habitat: Cleared woodland, especially rides and glades, railway embankments and fields bordering woods

On the wing: May – June and late July – mid-August as a second brood in favourable years

Adult: At rest, the Wood White's wings are never opened, and so only the undersides are seen, which are white, dusted with grey and yellow scales. The upper wing-surface of both sexes is white, with black apical patches on the forewings. Females have rounder forewings and any black patches are generally fainter. In the male, these patches are darker in the summer brood, whereas they may be totally absent in females of this second generation.

Life cycle: The pale-cream, keeled eggs are laid singly on the underside of the leaves of meadow vetchling, bitter vetch and tufted vetch, and hatch within seven days. The caterpillars rarely move far from the plant of their birth until ready to pupate. They are green with yellow side stripes, daytime feeders who rest along the margins of the

74

leaves. There they are easily found during July, when fully grown. By contrast, the green-and-pink chrysalis is difficult to find, attached by a silken girdle to vegetation near the original foodplant. The butterfly hibernates through the winter in the pupal stage, emerging the following May.

Observation and behaviour: Close observation of these butterflies reveals how delicate they are, as they flutter slowly and weakly just above the ground. Males can be seen patrolling woodland rides in an attempt to find an unmated female. They breed in discrete colonies which can consist of thousands of adults, but these are few and far between and the butterfly is unable to disperse to new sites. Good weather conditions are important for the successful life cycle of this species, with the larvae developing more quickly, and therefore forming more pupae, whenever rainfall is minimal. Female Wood Whites prefer to lay their eggs on foodplants growing just above neighbouring vegetation. However, the plants have to be growing in the right spot with both shade and sunlight; eggs and larvae survive best in woodland sites with about thirty per cent shade. Flying up and down the clearings and rides, the female Wood White is often to be seen searching for these ideal conditions.

Distribution: The Wood White is absent from Scotland, rare in Wales and localized in England. Less than one hundred sites are known, confined to the Midlands, east Wales, the Wealds of Sussex and Surrey, Hampshire, Wiltshire and Dorset. In both Devon and Somerset coastal colonies have been discovered, and elsewhere colonies have become established along disused railway embankments. Nearly half of all the English colonies exist in young conifer plantations where their future is uncertain, for once the trees are more than eight years old, their shade is too dense for the butterflies' survival. In Ireland, where the butterfly is still encouragingly common, it tends to inhabit widespread scrubland. The Irish sub-species (*juvernica*) has an obvious olive-green flush to the under wing-surfaces.

PALE CLOUDED YELLOW
Colias hyale

Wingspan: 48 mm (♂), 52 mm (♀)   **Status:** RM

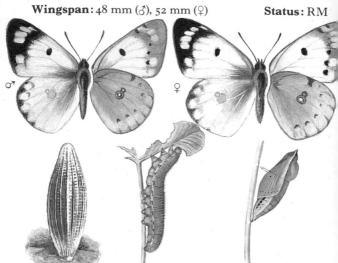

Typical habitat: Hillsides, clifftops and grassland wherever flowers are common

On the wing: May – September, in a single brood in good summers

Adult: The primrose-yellow upper wing-surfaces of the male are obvious when seen in flight, but the females, whose wings are almost white on the upperside, resemble the *helice* form of the ordinary Clouded Yellow (see page 78). Both sexes have a black apex and margin to the forewings, black margins on the hindwing upper surfaces, and a black spot in the middle of the forewings. They are difficult to tell apart from the Clouded Yellow, because the wing undersides, normally seen when the butterfly is at rest, are so similar. However the black forewing margins of the Pale Clouded Yellow don't continue around the inner edges of the wings as they do in the Clouded Yellow.

Life cycle: The eggs darken to red-orange, after being individually laid on bird's-foot-trefoil, clover or lucerne. Similar to the larva of the Clouded Yellow, the caterpillar is green and reddish-yellow and difficult to see on the foodplant. It is the uncertainty of our summer weather which prevents this species from completing its life cycle. If the summer is cold or wet, the caterpillar is unable to feed and so dies. Under favourable conditions, it will reach full size and pupate, forming a greenish-yellow pupa with darker green wing cases. The pupa is fixed in true girdle form to the foodplant or nearby vegetation. Hatching within seventeen days, the butterfly flies during August and September, but the eggs it lays and any caterpillars which may hatch are destined to perish as autumn approaches. It is doubtful whether any larvae have ever successfully hibernated in this country.

Observation and behaviour: As a typical migratory butterfly, the flight of the Pale Clouded Yellow is fast and powerful, but unlike the ordinary Clouded Yellow, it never disperses into northern Britain. The butterfly breeds throughout Southern Europe and gradually moves north into central Europe as the summer advances, where it breeds on the coastline of Germany and Holland. In southern Europe a third brood occurs, but only rarely does any generation reach Britain. Any butterflies which do arrive then fly across grassland looking for rich flower meadows.

Distribution: Most glimpses of this species occur on the South Downs and southern coastline. Numbers have never been so high as those of 1868, when the butterfly arrived in swarms, or 1900, when over 2,000 individual sightings were reported. One or two sightings in southern England occur most years, but there is a possibility that some of these are misidentifications of the more common *helice* form of Clouded Yellow. Although it reaches Ireland in good migration years, the Pale Clouded Yellow is absent from Scotland and the Isle of Man.

CLOUDED YELLOW
Colias croceus

Wingspan: 57 mm (♂), 62 mm (♀)   **Status:** SM

Typical habitat: Hillsides, coarse grasslands, clover and lucerne fields

On the wing: May – September. Upon arrival there is a single generation, which is unable to survive our winters.

Adult: Both sexes perch with wings held closed, so only the wing undersides can be closely examined. These are deep yellow, with a pinky-brown figure eight in the middle of the hindwing and a black spot on the forewing. The bright-orange upper wing-surfaces constantly flicker when the butterfly is observed in rapid flight and there are black marginal bands on all the wings. A pale form of the female, called *helice*, appears some years, with grey-white upper wing surfaces instead of orange.

Life cycle: The life cycle can only be studied when 'Clouded Yellow years' occur, during which the butterfly arrives from the Mediterranean in its hundreds or thousands. When the eggs are first laid on the upper surfaces of clover, bird's-foot-trefoil or, rarely in this country, lucerne, they are yellow, rapidly turning orange within a few days. Egg-laying begins in June and the eggs hatch after seven days. The resulting caterpillar is difficult to find on the foodplant. When fully grown it is dark green, with a yellow-and-orange marked line running through the spiracles. Rarely found because of its concealment in vegetation, the yellow-green chrysalis is of the girdled form and hatches within two or three weeks. Since there is no hibernation stage, the Clouded Yellow is unable to survive our winter, requiring a constant supply of larval foodplant. Those butterflies emerging in late July and August eventually meet with certain death as the temperatures drop; any eggs, larvae or pupae are killed by the first frosts.

Observation and behaviour: The powerful flight of this migratory butterfly allows it to reach Britain from the Mediterranean strongholds where it breeds in the winter. In spring, the new generation migrates north throughout Europe, reaching Britain in variable numbers most years, where it will breed. Sometimes the English visitors actually migrate further north across Scotland, but overall, sightings of this species are not as regular as those of other migrants, like the Red Admiral.

Distribution: This varies considerably according to the number of Clouded Yellows arriving each year, but because they are non-colonial, they may be seen anywhere. Generally, these butterflies are most likely to be found in southern England and the south coast of Ireland, where the influx first arrives. The South Downs during late summer are usually a good hunting-ground. 1947 was an unrivalled year, in which over 36,000 Clouded Yellows were officially recorded. More recently, 1983 was considered a 'Clouded Yellow year', during which numerous sightings occurred, in warm sheltered coombes and hillside valleys across southern Britain.

BERGER'S CLOUDED YELLOW
Colias australis

Wingspan: 50 mm (♂), 52 mm (♀)　　　　　**Status:** RM

Typical habitat: Chalkhills and downland
On the wing: June – September
Adult: This butterfly is almost impossible to distinguish from the Pale Clouded Yellow, of which at one time it was thought to be a subspecies. In 1947 the Belgian lepidopterist, L. A. Berger, identified it as a separate species, because not only did the caterpillars look different, they also fed on different foodplants. Berger's Clouded Yellow is the brighter yellow of the two species, with a more distinct bright orange dot on the upper surface of the hindwings. Additionally, the black border on the hindwing upper

surface is much reduced in this species, but can only be examined once the butterfly has been captured.

Life cycle: The orange-red eggs are laid on horseshoe vetch when the butterfly arrives in June. As with the Pale Clouded Yellow, the green caterpillars, with distinctive yellow stripes and black dots, will pupate if the weather is favourable and hatch into a summer brood of butterflies. This brood mate and lay eggs towards late summer, but the resulting caterpillars (which would normally hibernate whilst small) are unable to survive the cold temperatures of a typical British winter. The life cycle can therefore rarely be completed in the wild. The pupae are light green with pale-yellow dorsal and lateral markings and are of the girdled type.

Observation and behaviour: The swift flight of this butterfly resembles that of the Pale Clouded Yellow, but because of the distribution of the larval foodplant, it generally flies across chalk downland and rough grassland.

Distribution: This is by far the rarest of the three Clouded Yellows visiting Britain. Berger's Clouded Yellow breeds throughout western and central Europe and is widespread in Portugal, Spain, Germany and France. It migrates to Holland, Belgium, Denmark and southern England. No observations have ever been recorded in Ireland or Scandinavia, but it is possible the butterfly is frequently overlooked because of its similarity to the Pale Clouded Yellow.

BRIMSTONE
Gonepteryx rhamni

Wingspan: 60 mm (♂ and ♀)   **Status:** R

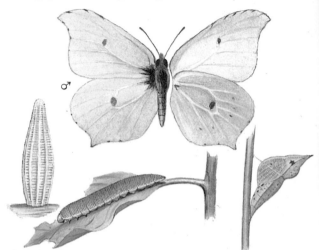

Typical habitat: Woodland margins, glades, hedgerows and grassy scrubland

On the wing: February – October in a single brood

Adult: The males are bright yellow on the upper wing-surface, with an orange spot on each wing; the underside of both wings is duller, with pale-brown spots. The antennae are noticeably pink. Females are much paler on the upper wing-surfaces with a green tinge and in flight, may be confused with the Large White. It is believed by some people that the word 'butterfly' derives from a description of the male of this species – the butter-yellow Brimstone. When at rest, both sexes hold their wings closed and their outline shape is unique.

Life cycle: Towards the middle of May and throughout June, the bottle-shaped eggs are laid singly on the underside of buckthorn leaves and towards the shoot tips. Both common and alder buckthorn are used, and female Brimstones have the ability to locate these small shrubs amongst all the other bushes along wood margins. Within ten days the eggs hatch and the pale-yellow caterpillars turn green after the first moult. They sit along the midrib on the upper surface of the leaf and are easy to find because of the clear feeding damage around them. After one month a pale-green, perfectly-camouflaged, girdled pupa is formed on the buckthorn twig or on other vegetation. The butterflies, which emerge in August, will eventually hibernate through the winter.

Observation and behaviour: The male Brimstone, emerging from hibernation deep in ivy or bramble bushes, is the first butterfly on the wing each spring. Both sexes are long-lived, probably reaching eleven or twelve months, but half of this span is spent in hibernation. During mild winters they waken and take short flights before returning to hibernation. The butterflies are very active in spring, with males patrolling for females whom they mate almost immediately after hibernation. Those males emerging first in spring have a better chance of finding an unmated female. In summer, male and female butterflies emerge from the pupae at the same time. They totally ignore the chance to mate and spend all their time avidly feeding on thistle, teasel and willowherbs before entering hibernation.

Distribution: The availability of the foodplant determines the distribution of this butterfly. Common buckthorn, on which the Brimstone feeds, is found wherever limestone occurs, but both species of buckthorn are rare in Scotland. Alder buckthorn is localized in Ireland. Southern England, and as far north as the Humber Estuary, is the real stronghold for this species, with the most northerly sites in Cumbria. Isolated colonization occurs in Wales.

LARGE WHITE
Pieris brassicae

Wingspan: 63 mm (♂), 70 mm (♀)

Status: R

Summer
brood

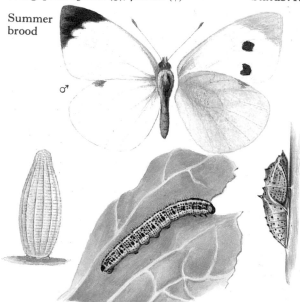

♂

Typical habitat: Virtually all types of countryside, especially near cabbages

On the wing: May – September in two distinct broods

Adult: The pure white upper wing-surfaces of this butterfly are common to both sexes. The forewings have black tips, and the female also has two black spots in the middle of these wings. The undersides have no markings, but are light yellow, powdered with grey flecks.

Life cycle: Most people will have seen at some time the yellow bottle-shaped eggs of the Large White, laid in orderly batches on both sides of cabbage leaves from May to September. Within a week they will have hatched. The pale-green larvae eventually turn grey-green, patterned with yellow-and-black markings and bearing short white hairs. They feed in groups on cabbages and other cultivated brassicae, or nasturtiums, and eventually strip the leaves to a mere skeleton. The larvae always have an unpleasant smell about them. Leaving the foodplant after a month to pupate, the grey-green chrysalis is attached to a fence, house wall, or tree trunk in typical girdled fashion. Those of the first generation hatch within two weeks, but late summer pupae overwinter to hatch in May.

Observation and behaviour: Although its flight is sometimes hovering or fluttering, this species is a powerful flier and is even migratory in certain years. Our British populations are frequently reinforced by continental immigrants. With a nomadic lifestyle, the Large White may be found anywhere, breeding wherever the habitat is suitable, but especially near vegetable gardens and allotments. Cabbages and brussel sprouts are the favourite larval foodplants. In fact, the Large White and the Small White, whose caterpillars feed on the same foodplants, are often referred to as 'Cabbage Whites'; they are the only species in Britain significantly damaging to commercial crops. Fortunately, biological pest control is performed by parasitic braconid wasps, which lay eggs on the caterpillar prior to pupation. These eggs hatch into grubs which feed on the living caterpillar, eventually accounting for a ninety per cent death rate each season. Additionally, the chalcid wasp preys on the butterfly at the pupal stage, actually laying its eggs inside the chrysalis before it hardens fully. The grubs devour the chrysalis from the inside, outwards.

Distribution: The Large White is found throughout the British Isles from the Shetlands to the Scillies and is one of our most common species. It is found in all counties in a variety of habitats, even in mountainous country at high altitudes. In some years, for reasons unknown, this species has occurred in plague proportions, but this has not happened for some while.

SMALL WHITE
Pieris rapae

Wingspan: 48 mm (♂ and ♀)   **Status:** R

Summer
brood

Typical habitat: Any habitat and countryside, but especially sheltered land by cabbages

On the wing: March – mid-May and mid-June – August in two distinct broods. In favourable years, a third brood is possible during September/October.

Adult: Both sexes have white upper wings. The male has black tips and a single black spot on the forewings, whereas the female has two black spots. Females also have an additional grey-black streak on the lower edge of the forewings. In the spring brood, any black markings tend to be greyer. The wing undersides are similar in both sexes, with a yellow apex to the white forewings and black dots, but the hindwing undersides are yellow.

Life cycle: The yellow, typically bottle-shaped, eggs are laid singly on the underside of cabbages, from April onwards. Alternatively, when commercial crops are not present, wild plants of the *Cruciferae* family, such as wild mignonette, garlic mustard and hedge mustard, are used.

Unlike the Large White, the Small White caterpillar, which hatches inside a week, is solitary and chews its way right into the heart of the cabbage, where it feeds. When it finally emerges fully grown, it is dark green, and blends perfectly with the leaf midrib on which it rests. The chrysalis is variable and may be light-brown or green, with darker speckles. Pupae of the first brood are usually formed on the foodplant, but second brood larvae pupate on tree trunks, in hedges or on buildings and fences, where they overwinter.

Observation and behaviour: As with the Large White, this species is a serious pest to cabbages and related vegetables, but prefers those growing in a sheltered environment. For this reason, crops in gardens, where the vegetables are grown close to a hedge or fence, are more prone to damage than commercial crops in open fields. Colonies are not formed, but the butterflies wander throughout the countryside, egg-laying wherever the foodplants are available. They are frequently seen in small groups or pairs. Each year the resident population is reinforced by continental migrants and when the large, second brood of residents emerge, overall numbers are high.

Distribution: This very common butterfly is found nearly everywhere throughout Ireland, Wales, southern Scotland and England. It is rare or absent in the Hebrides and on Shetland. Other islands, including the Isle of Man, Anglesey and the Scillies are, however, colonized.

GREEN-VEINED WHITE
Pieris napi

Wingspan: 50 mm (♂ and ♀) **Status:** R

Spring brood

♀

Typical habitat: Damp meadows, riverbanks, shaded hedgerows and woodland margins

On the wing: April – September in two distinct broods

Adult: The markings and their intensity can vary between the two broods of Green-veined Whites, but the upper wing-surfaces are always white. Males show a black apex, single black spot and black veins on the forewings, and one black spot on the costal margin of the hindwing. The markings on the female are more intense, with an extra black spot on the forewing. All the markings are fainter in the spring brood, as shown in this female illustrated. The wing undersides of both sexes are similar; the yellow hindwing undersides with veins bordered in grey-black give the butterfly its name. They create the optical illusion of appearing green against the yellow scales.

Life cycle: In May, the bottle-shaped, yellow eggs are laid singly on the underside of the leaves of wild, cabbage-related plants, such as cuckoo flower, charlock and garlic mustard. Unlike the Large and Small Whites, this closely-related species does not affect crops. In less than a week the eggs hatch and after the first moult, the caterpillar is green with yellow circles around the spiracles. Keen observation will reveal it feeding on the leaves and stems. The green or buff chrysalis is more difficult to find, attached by a silken girdle in dense vegetation. Pupae of the spring generation hatch inside two weeks, whereas those of the summer brood hibernate through the winter.

Observation and behaviour: This species does not show the migratory behaviour of the Large White, but despite its weak, erratic flight, it is quite mobile, breeding and feeding wherever ideal conditions occur. The butterflies are loosely colonial, especially in the northern part of the range, and the second brood is the larger, with hundreds of adults flying during August. The Green-veined White is unusual because it will fly on dull, overcast days, providing the air temperature is high enough. When resting, it frequently holds its wings half-open, and it can be approached feeding from wetland flowers in sunshine. Despite favouring a shaded and damp habitat, in some parts of Britain it successfully colonizes open moorland.

Distribution: This is one of the most common butterflies in Britain, absent only from the northern Highlands and the Shetlands. Preferring damp conditions, it was affected by the 1976 drought, but today is extremely widespread despite its habitat being drained, and thus destroyed, for agricultural development. Around Donegal in Ireland, a characteristically darker subspecies is also found.

ORANGE-TIP
Anthocharis cardamines

Wingspan: 45 mm (♂), 50 mm (♀)

Status: R

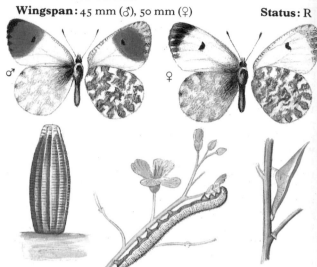

Typical habitat: Open woodland, hedgerows, grass verges and damp meadows

On the wing: May – June in a single brood

Adult: The male Orange-tip can be easily recognized, with its white upper wing-surfaces, dusted with black near the body, and orange tips to the forewings. The female, with black tips to the forewings instead of orange, is less identifiable and is sometimes mistaken for a Green-veined White or Small White. The hindwing undersides are similar in both sexes, showing a beautiful, mottled, green-yellow pattern, which perfectly camouflages the butterfly when resting on the flowers of garlic mustard.

Life cycle: From May to June the bottle-shaped eggs, which turn orange a few days after being laid, are easy to find underneath flowerbuds of garlic mustard, hedge mustard, honesty, charlock and cuckoo flower. They hatch within a week. The caterpillars eat each other during the early stages of growth, and this is the main reason why butterflies will not lay eggs on a flower-head already bearing an egg. The developing caterpillars spend their entire life on the one plant, eating the flowers and later the seed capsules, with which they blend perfectly when fully grown. With their long, thin bodies, bluey-white upper surfaces and dark-green lower ones, the caterpillars are easy to find by careful searching during June and July. When fully grown they wander from the foodplant to pupate in dense undergrowth. The pale-brown or green pupae are difficult to locate. They hibernate through the winter suspended by a girdle to stems or twigs.

Observation and behaviour: Like many members of the *Pieridae*, or Whites family, the Orange-tip is a roaming species, not confined to particular colonies. The males may be observed doubling back on their flightpath in search of flowers for nectar, or an unmated female. They are active only whilst the sun shines, when they regularly stop to bask with wings wide open. Both sexes fly commonly where the larval foodplants thrive. Cuckoo flower is found in damp low-lying meadows or woodland rides on heavy soils, whereas garlic mustard grows along hedgerows, wood margins or wasteland where the soil is drier and calcareous. Although these major foodplants support populations of the butterfly across a wide distribution, many damp meadows have been drained and hedgerows grubbed out, as farming methods change.

Distribution: Throughout Wales and Ireland, the Orange-tip is still a common butterfly. Apart from parts of the North-East, it is also common throughout England, despite some decline due to habitat destruction. Early in the last century the butterfly was common in most of Scotland, but today it is largely absent from southern Scotland, the Highlands and the offshore islands. Only in north-east Scotland are populations strong, and recent surveys indicate that the species may well be colonizing new areas in this region.

GREEN HAIRSTREAK
Callophrys rubi
Wingspan: 33 mm (♂ and ♀)　　　　　　　　**Status:** R

Typical habitat: Rough scrubland and grassland, chalk downland, moors, lowland heaths and woodland margins
On the wing: May – June in a single brood
Adult: Both sexes are very similar, with brown upper wing-surfaces and bright-green undersides. The green under-surfaces are regularly seen because this butterfly always perches with wings closed. They are edged with orange-brown margins and a variably clear, white, broken line transverses both wings. The antennae perfectly resemble miniature belisha beacons.
Life cycle: Small colonies of this butterfly occur in a variety of habitats, the flattened green eggs being laid singly on a range of foodplants, depending on the locality. Constant features of most of the sites are the presence of shrubs and a warm and sheltered aspect. Foodplant shrubs include gorse, broom, buckthorn (berries) and dogwood (buds). Bilberry is made use of on moorland, rock-rose and bird's-foot-trefoil on calcareous grassland, and dyer's greenweed on other grassland habitats. Within a week the egg hatches, and after the first moult the caterpillar becomes white with brown stripes. When fully grown, after the third moult, it is green with yellow stripes,

making it difficult to find on certain foodplants. After the first moult, the caterpillar is extremely solitary, since it is fiercely cannibalistic. Towards the middle of summer, it crawls to the ground and forms the brown pupa, which is difficult to find.

Observation and behaviour: The Green Hairstreak is the only British butterfly with distinctly green scales and since it is on the wing when shrubs and hedges are in early leaf, it can be perfectly invisible when at rest. Once disturbed, it is difficult to track, as it takes off in rapid, jerky flight. However, since the male in particular is territorial, and always has a favourite south-facing perching spot, it is purely a question of waiting for the butterfly to return. Territorial perches are frequently in hedgerow shrubs with overhanging branches. Each shrub will only conceal one male, who investigates any passing butterfly in anticipation of finding a female. Females fly across more open countryside, looking for egg-laying sites, but may sometimes be observed being chased by a male in courtship flights, or feeding on the flowers of bird's-foot-trefoil and rock-rose. Both sexes visit the wayfaring tree flowers for nectar and honeydew on the leaves.

Distribution: This butterfly is the most common of our five Hairstreaks, despite many of its sites being destroyed in the last forty years by grassland reclamation and agricultural development of heaths, moors and bogland. It remains common in southern England, especially on chalk and limestone, the West Country, Wales, the Midlands and eastern England, with strong colonies also throughout Scotland and coastal Ireland. As the countryside continues to be developed and 'tidied up', the Green Hairstreak will undoubtedly decline, but so far it remains a familiar sight in those of its habitats which are still undisturbed.

BROWN HAIRSTREAK
Thecla betulae

Wingspan: 38 mm (♂), 40 mm (♀)   **Status:** R

Typical habitat: Woodland margins and hedgerows close to woods

On the wing: August – September in a single brood

Adult: The upper wing-surface of both sexes is brown, but the female is darker and bears distinct orange patches on the forewings, which are replaced by pale blotches in the male. Orange markings appear on the hindwing upper surfaces, near the small tails, and again these are brighter in the female. The wing undersides of both sexes are more striking, with the pale-orange base colour marked with white stripes, black lines and red bands, correspondingly richer in the female.

Life cycle: During autumn, when leaves have fallen from the trees, and spring, the squat white eggs are easily found. They are attached singly or in pairs to the twigs of blackthorn, which is the only larval foodplant, and are laid during August and September below the blackthorn spines or in the forks of branching twigs. They overwinter before hatching in early May, if they have survived spring hedge-trimming. Resembling a miniature slug, the green and yellow caterpillar is most easily found in June, when it hides underneath the blackthorn leaves, with its head pointing downwards. It is marvellously camouflaged, but once one is spotted, the patient observer will eventually locate many more, since colonies of the butterfly are generally compact. However, the dark-brown pupa is hard to find, formed deep in leaf litter on the ground.

Observation and behaviour: Brown Hairstreaks are elusive butterflies and are rarely seen, because they spend most of their time high in the tree canopy where they feed on aphid honeydew. They are sedentary, with the small colonies confined to the same woodlands each year. Courtship and mating take place high in the branches of a favourite 'master tree', frequently ash or oak. Males rarely descend to the woodland floor and most sightings are of females, laying their eggs in the neighbouring hedgerows. The eggs are laid some distance from where the butterflies mated. Although typically, both sexes perch with their wings closed, after laying her eggs, the female opens her wings, revealing the russet orange patches. These camouflage markings help blend the vulnerable egg-laying female with the hedgerow, at a time when orange and red berries such as those of the hawthorn, are present. Even though the butterflies fly late in the year, they are still only active during sunny weather; temperatures below 19°C cause the adults to roost. They feed avidly on bramble blossom and a secretion from ash trees.

Distribution: The Brown Hairstreak has always been a scarce butterfly, with between 100 and 150 colonies left in Britain today. In Scotland and northern England it is extinct and seems to be confined to the Burren of County Clare in Ireland. The remaining localities are generally those with heavy soils, especially clays, and mature hedgerows and woodland nearby. It is extinct in East Anglia.

PURPLE HAIRSTREAK
Quercusia quercus
Wingspan: 37 mm (♀), 39 mm (♂)   **Status:** R

Typical habitat: Oakwoods or large single oak trees
On the wing: July – September in a single brood
Adult: The ground colour of the upper wing-surfaces is a
blue-black, parts of which turn vivid purple when sunlight
catches the wings at certain angles. Only a small forewing
patch on the female reacts in this way, but in the male, the
entire upper wing-surface, except the margins, turns
purple. The undersides of both wings are light grey,
camouflaging the butterflies perfectly when viewed
against the sky in the canopy. They are marked with a
white line and orange spots towards the hindwing tails.
Life cycle: The eggs are laid singly on twigs of the sessile
or pedunculate oaks, near the base of a flower bud or on a
fork between two twigs. They overwinter in this stage.
Being grey-white they are easily found by close examination in winter. When the leaves break in April, the egg
hatches and the small caterpillar eats into the expanding
buds. As it grows, it spins a silken web which holds the
disintegrating bud and leaves together. It is a nocturnal

feeder, grazing on the oak leaves and returning to the web during the daytime. This web usually traps the brown scale leaves which would normally fall to the ground, and since the caterpillar is brown and segmented, these trapped scales provide it with ideal camouflage. After seven weeks the caterpillar is full-grown and descends to the woodland floor, where the red-brown pupa is formed among the leaf litter and is virtually impossible to find.

Observation and behaviour: Like so many of the Hairstreaks this is an elusive butterfly, preferring to spend its time in the upper branches of oak trees, where aphid honeydew forms its main adult food. Sometimes it flies to the woodland floor to feed on nectar from creeping thistles and other flowers. The isolated colonies vary annually in size and in good years hundreds of butterflies fly around the treetops. Significant aerial activity occurs during sunny weather between 3 and 7 p.m., when the butterflies fly around the oak trees, landing on lower branches between one and two metres above the ground. Here they bask with open wings, and can be most easily seen. Females have a specific egg-laying period between noon and 3 p.m., but only during warm weather. They also visit the lower branches during these times of day. The ideal woodland habitat will have both oak and ash trees, because males prefer to roost and perch on ash leaves, ready to intercept a passing female. Copulation also takes place in ash trees, though females then disperse to lay their eggs on neighbouring oak twigs. Wherever large colonies occur, both these species of tree are present.

Distribution: Rare in northern Britain and very localized in Ireland, the Purple Hairstreak is probably more common than people realize elsewhere in England. South of the Wash, it colonizes most woods wherever oak is established, and it is found throughout Wales. Despite the fact that many good sites have been destroyed as oak trees are replaced by conifer plantations, small colonies are found wherever occasional oaks grow, including copses, parks, large gardens and stately homes throughout southern England.

WHITE-LETTER HAIRSTREAK
Strymonidia w-album

Wingspan: 36 mm (♂ and ♀)

Status: R

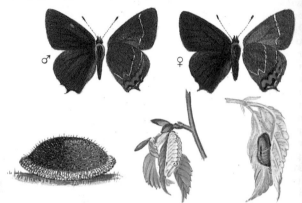

Typical habitat: Woodland margins and hedgerows near elm trees

On the wing: July – August in a single brood

Adult: Females have longer tails on the hindwings than males, but in other respects the sexes are similar. The upper wing-surfaces are blackish-brown but they are hardly ever seen clearly, because the wings are always held closed when the butterfly is not in flight. A characteristic white, W-shaped line runs across the dark-brown underside of both wings, and orange crescents adorn the margin of the hindwings. Unlike the similar Black Hairstreak, there are no black dots next to the orange markings on the hindwings.

Life cycle: During July, the brown-and-white eggs are laid singly below flower buds on the twigs of elm trees facing the sun. The eggs overwinter, hatching in early March. The young caterpillars feed on elm flowers, before chewing their way into leaf buds and eventually feeding on unfolded leaves. Fully grown, they are bright green and rest on the upper surface of the leaves, close to the mid-rib. The dark-brown pupa looks quite unusual, covered in numerous hairs, and is attached to the hairy twigs for protection until the butterfly emerges about a month later.

Observation and behaviour: The White-letter Hairstreak is seldom seen because it rarely flies, preferring to crawl around the tree tops, feeding on aphid honeydew and basking. It generally has a favourite perching branch, which does not necessarily have to be in an elm tree; oaks are popular alternatives. If observed flying, its movements are jerky and gyratory. Sometimes it descends to feed on bramble, creeping thistle and privet, and this is when it can best be seen. Females are particularly active in warm weather, dispersing throughout the canopy to lay their eggs at all levels in the trees.

Distribution: Always having been confined to particular areas, numbers of this butterfly have seriously declined since Dutch elm disease killed most of the common and wych elms in the 1970s. Populations were always confined to groups of elms, or even an isolated hedgerow tree, and colonies were strongest in the Midlands, southern England and throughout Wales. Today, the Hairstreak is rare everywhere. Elm suckers provide the only source of food throughout most of its range, where small but diminishing colonies continue to survive. Suckers have a limited life because, as they are attached to the trunk of the original tree, they continue to be infected through the roots, and die before exceeding four metres. The White-letter Hairstreak is faring better in the north of its range, where wych elm survives. However, the long-term future of this elusive, specialized butterfly is far from good, especially as it has declined throughout Europe too, because of the loss of its foodplant.

BLACK HAIRSTREAK
Strymonidia pruni

Wingspan: 37 mm (♂ and ♀)   **Status:** R

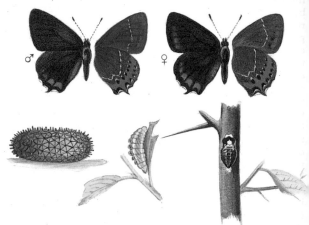

Typical habitat: Sheltered woodland edges, rides and glades

On the wing: Late June – July in a single brood

Adult: The wings of this butterfly are always held closed, so the dark-brown upper surfaces with orange marginal patches are never seen. The wing undersides of both sexes are golden brown, with a distinct orange marginal band on the hindwings which sometimes continues on to the forewings. This band is marked with black and white, and there is a broken W-shaped white line traversing both wings, which sometimes causes the Black Hairstreak to be confused with the White-letter Hairstreak.

Life cycle: The eggs of this species are laid singly, beneath a fork on a blackthorn branch, during July. Young and old blackthorn bushes are the only shrubs used for egg-laying. The eggs resemble squashed discs and are orange-brown, covered in fine projections. Having overwintered, towards late March they hatch, the caterpillar showing a characteristic black head and brown body. After the first moult, some segments turn green, although most stay brown. However after the third moult, when full size is reached, the body is pale green with yellow stripes and pink dorsal ridges. This perfect camouflage enables the caterpillar to conceal itself on newly formed buds or on the new leaves. Even the black-and-white chrysalis is easily overlooked because it perfectly mimics a bird dropping. It is formed on the upper leaf surface or along a twig of blackthorn.

Observation and behaviour: Because the early stages of this species are so well-concealed and the adults are retiring by nature, the Black Hairstreak is frequently overlooked. It remains high in the oak canopy or at the top of blackthorn bushes, where it feeds on aphid honeydew. In warm weather, both sexes descend to the woodland floor to drink nectar from wild privet and bramble, their favourite foodplants, and this is the best time to observe them. The discrete, small colonies inhabit specific areas of an overall larger habitat. The eggs are laid on foodplant not shaded more than 75 per cent by the canopy; mature hedges along woodland margins are ideal. A mosaic of warm, sheltered blackthorn thickets, privet bushes and glades within a larger wood is the prime breeding habitat for this sedentary butterfly.

Distribution: This rare butterfly has been recorded on less than eighty sites since its discovery in 1828. Apart from one colony in Surrey, the species occupies a belt from Peterborough, south as far as Oxford, occurring in ancient woodland on low-lying clays. These sites mark the northern-most limit of its European range, where about thirty known colonies exist. The East Midland woodlands in which the butterflies are to be found were managed for centuries on long coppice cycles, with small scrub areas being cut each year on a twenty-year rotation. Most other British woods were managed on an eight-to-fifteen-year cycle, which disturbed the butterfly's habitat.

LARGE COPPER
Lycaena dispar batavus

Wingspan: 40 mm (♂), 42 mm (♀)

Status: R
(*reintroduced*)

Typical habitat: Fenland and dyke margins
On the wing: July in a single brood
Adult: Our own Large Copper (*L. dispar dispar*) once thrived on the fens of Cambridgeshire and Somerset, but because of drainage of the habitat for arable land and over-collecting, it became extinct in 1857. A closely-related Dutch species (*L. dispar batavus*) was introduced in 1927 and now survives on one site in Cambridgeshire. The male of this butterfly has metallic flame-red upper wing-surfaces, with black margins and white fringes. Even more attractive are the undersides, where the hindwings are tinged pale blue, marked with black spots and orange marginal bands, and the forewings are pale orange, adorned with black dots with white haloes. The female is similarly marked on the underside, but the upper wing-

surfaces have additional black spots and wider black wing margins.

Life cycle: Great water-dock is the only larval foodplant of the Large Copper, and in July and early August the greeny-white eggs are laid singly, or in groups of up to four, on both surfaces of the leaves. Plants away from the water's edge surrounded by other aquatic vegetation are favourite sites for egg-laying. Within ten days the eggs hatch and the pale-yellow caterpillar immediately crawls to the underside of the leaf, where it nibbles a groove in the surface in which to rest. After the first moult it turns green, and during the second instar it hibernates, turning pinkish-red. Hibernation occurs deep in decaying ground vegetation, and during winter the caterpillar can survive prolonged submersion while the fen is flooded. Towards the end of March, feeding recommences and the larva's colour reverts to green, before it starts to form the brown-and-white pupa on nearby vegetation.

Observation and behaviour: The extinction of the British Large Copper was partly caused by the decline in management systems on the fenlands, whereby reeds are regularly cut and harvested to control their growth. The butterfly only selects great water-dock for egg-laying because it is easily accessible, ignoring those plants heavily overgrown. Habitat conditions affect the size of the annual breeding population, because if the fens flood during the summer both the larvae and foodplant are submerged when feeding should be taking place.

Distribution: The fens flooded in 1968, so that in 1969 the population had dropped to extinction level and required the intervention of artificially-controlled breeding programmes. Livestock was reared in captivity and released to maintain numbers in 1970. During 1984 and 1985, numbers of free-flying adults had once again reached low levels and in the summer of 1987, over 1,000 adults were released to retain a wild population. The Nature Conservancy Reserve at Wood Walton Fen, Cambridgeshire, is the only protected site where the Large Copper has been reintroduced.

SMALL COPPER

Lycaena phlaeas

Wingspan: 32 mm (♂), 35 mm (♀)   **Status:** R

Typical habitat: Unimproved rough grassland, including hillsides, wasteland, clifftops and woodland rides

On the wing: April – October in three possible broods, especially in southern England

Adult: The butterfly is easy to identify because the sexes are similar and both have brilliant copper-orange upper wing-surfaces, with black borders and dots. Equally characteristic, the undersides of the forewings are pale orange with black dots and the hindwings are grey-brown. The butterfly can be extremely variable throughout its range, especially in the amount of black on the wings. Another variation, more common in Scotland, shows blue spots on the hindwing uppersides.

Life cycle: Common sorrel, sheep's sorrel and various docks are the main larval foodplants, on which the miniature golfball-like eggs are laid, on the upper surface near the central midrib. Hatching within a week, the small larvae eat grooves into the underside of the leaf, disclosing their whereabouts. Feeding occurs during the daytime, even during rain showers. The caterpillars' colour can be variable after the first moult; some are light green, whereas others are green with pink stripes. Both forms are well camouflaged on the foodplant. They rest beneath the leaves and pupate after a month, although those of the third brood enter hibernation in October. The pale-brown, darker-speckled pupa is difficult to find, lying deep in leaf litter or attached to the foodplant by a silken girdle. It hatches within four weeks.

Observation and behaviour: The discrete colonies of this active butterfly are often small and usually only occupy limited areas, such as a sunspot along the margins of a wood. They are not confined to grassland and are found in places where the soil is bare, such as quarry faces and trackways, but always where nectar-producing flowers grow close by. Favourite flowers include common ragwort, marjoram, knapweeds and thistles. Grass stems are used for roosting. The Small Coppers adore basking, and in late summer and autumn will perch on fleabane, where they rest with wings held in a half-open position. Males are highly territorial, selecting an area with bare soil and stones where they can bask, but with vantage perches from which to defend their territory. Any wandering butterfly is rapidly approached and chased away, unless it is an unmated female. Even birds are attacked if they perch too close to a territory-defending male! During warm summers in southern counties, three broods are possible, with the first flight period in May/June and the last in September/October. Weather conditions certainly control egg-laying activity, since this only takes place in sunshine.

Distribution: Although the geographical range of the Small Copper has remained constant over the last century, populations have declined as heathlands have been reclaimed and grasslands lost to the plough. It is still, however, a common butterfly throughout the British Isles, but is not found on higher mountainous ground or on some of the offshore Scottish islands. Populations are found on the Isle of Man, Anglesey and the Isle of Wight, and throughout Ireland.

SMALL BLUE
Cupido minimus

Wingspan: 24 mm (♂ and ♀)　　　　　　　　　　**Status:** R

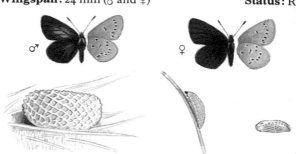

Typical habitat: South-facing downs, grassy slopes, quarries and embankments

On the wing: Mid-May – June in a single brood

Adult: Since this is Britain's smallest butterfly, it is easy to identify. The upper wing-surface of the male is sooty-black, powdered with silvery-blue scales near the body. Females are browner on the upper wing-surfaces and lack the blue scales. Both sexes have silver-grey undersides, flecked with black dots, which lack the typical orange spots found on other members of the Blue family.

Life cycle: The small, blue, disc-shaped eggs are laid singly between the fingers on the flower-head of kidney vetch during June; up to three eggs are deposited per flower-head. No other foodplant is used. After a week the eggs hatch, and the larvae remain on the flower-head, eating into the seedpods until they reach full size in late July. They are grub-like and pink-grey when fully grown, with their heads invariably buried in the seedpod. As August approaches, they leave the flower-head and enter hibernation. Surviving the winter low down in ground vegetation, the caterpillar remains fully grown for around eight months, before pupating the following May. The pupae are almost impossible to find. They are buff with black dots and striped wing cases, and are covered with fine hairs.

Observation and behaviour: The Small Blue prefers grassy hollows which trap the sun, but the colonies are extremely small and localized, consisting of a few dozen adults. Although kidney vetch has a wide distribution on calcareous soils, the butterfly is by no means found everywhere this plant grows. The colonies are confined to a few specific plants within restricted areas. Sometimes the same hundred or so plants are used from one year to the next, which demonstrates the sedentary habit of this species. The butterflies are rapid fliers and frequently visit flowers for nectar, especially trefoils and vetches, suggesting a penchant for yellow flowers. Neighbouring taller grasses and scrub vegetation are used by the butterflies as nocturnal roosts, and such plants are also selected by the males as territorial perches. Here they bask with wings held half-open, disappearing to intercept passing females before returning to the same perch.

Distribution: This minute butterfly is a very localized species, confined to chalk and limestone soils. Although it can be found in northern Scotland, it is more frequent in southern England. Warm, sheltered sunspots are always preferred; in Wales it appears restricted to the southern coastline. Kidney vetch is common on the coast in the West Country, but only a very few colonies of the butterfly are found there. The Cotswolds remain the prime stronghold, with some large colonies, but there has been a worrying decline in numbers there in recent years, caused by agricultural development and the permanent loss of downland habitats. The calcareous hills of Dorset, Hampshire and the Chilterns in Buckinghamshire all contain localized colonies. The butterflies are reluctant to disperse, and only fly from one hillside to another ideal site close by.

SILVER-STUDDED BLUE
Plebejus argus

Wingspan: 29 mm (♀), 31 mm (♂)   **Status:** R

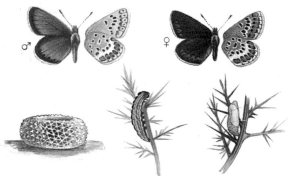

Typical habitat: Heathland, also sheltered limestone cliffs

On the wing: July – late August in a single brood

Adult: This is a variably-marked butterfly, differing between one colony and another, and there are distinct races and subspecies throughout its range. The description here refers to the typical heathland subspecies, *argus*, which is illustrated. Males have violet-blue upper wing-surfaces, with black borders and white fringes to all the wings. The undersides are silvery-blue with broad orange bands on the hindwings, edged with black crescents and dots. Each dot has a bright blue pupil, which is not found on any other Blue butterfly. Females have brown upper wing-surfaces, sometimes tinged blue near the body, and with a row of orange marginal dots on the hindwings which frequently continue into the forewings. They are so similar in markings to the Brown Argus, that close examination is necessary to distinguish between the two. The undersides resemble those of the male, but the ground colour is browner.

Life cycle: White disc-shaped eggs are laid singly in

summer on the woody shoots of gorse and bell heather, or bird's-foot-trefoil in limestone habitats. They overwinter until the following April, when they hatch. The larvae feed on the leaf cuticle before moving to the tender flower buds or new leaves. They are difficult to find as their green-and-brown markings provide good camouflage. However, as they are always surrounded by ants day and night, who milk their sugary secretion, these insects may reveal their location on the foodplant. The pale-brown pupa is formed at the base of the foodplant and is almost impossible to find, since it is either carried into the ants' nest, or buried underground by them to protect its sweet secretion. The pupa usually hatches within eighteen days.

Observation and behaviour: Numbers of this butterfly are swelled by the existence of different subspecies. Reluctant to colonize new sites, this butterfly is highly sedentary by nature. As a result, the discrete colonies, which can be very large, sometimes occupy only very small areas where conditions are suitable. These are frequently areas of heathland which has been burnt. Sparse, spindly areas of heather which are sheltered and catch the sunlight are preferred while well-established, mature heaths are ignored. Close views of the butterfly are best obtained when it is perching to mate on heather, or when feeding from thyme or marjoram. Roosting takes place on dead flower-heads or grass stems. At one time, the Silver-studded Blues colonized chalk downlands, but this form of the butterfly is now extinct and outside the heathland habitat, the species is confined to quarries and cliffs.

Distribution: Once found throughout much of Britain, the Silver-studded Blue is now largely restricted to heathlands in Dorset, Hampshire and Surrey, with smaller populations in Norfolk and Suffolk. Sand-dune colonies exist in Devon, Cornwall and South Wales, and the subspecies *caernensis* breeds on limestone cliffs around Great Orme in north Wales. Large populations also occur on Anglesey where limestone cliffs are the main haunt.

BROWN ARGUS
Aricia agestis

Wingspan: 29 mm (♂ and ♀)   **Status:** R

Typical habitat: Chalk and limestone grassland, rough hillsides and clifftops

On the wing: May – September in two distinct broods

Adult: Both sexes are similar, with dark-brown upper wing-surfaces, white marginal fringes and orange crescents around the edges of all the wings. Females are slightly paler brown, but the orange markings are larger and extend into the apex of the forewing. The undersides are greyish-brown, with black spots circled by white haloes, and both wings show obvious submarginal orange spots. Since no blue markings occur in this species, the butterflies can be distinguished from brown females of the Common Blue.

Life cycle: The white, disc-shaped eggs are easily recognizable. They are to be found on the underside of the leaves of rock-rose on chalk soils, and common storksbill on sandier soils, and hatch in a week. The small larvae perforate the underside of the leaf as they chew, but leave the upper transparent cuticle in place. As they develop, the caterpillars eat the entire leaf, feeding by daytime and well-camouflaged by their pale-green and pink markings. As with the Silver-studded Blue, ants always attend the larvae, milking them for their sugary secretion. The presence of ants often discloses their whereabouts. First-generation larvae pupate after six weeks, but those of the second brood hibernate after the second moult until the following April. The light-brown pupa is difficult to find because it is nearly always buried by ants. It hatches within two weeks.

Observation and behaviour: The small discrete colonies of the Brown Argus fluctuate in size each year. They are active in bright sunshine, and are sedentary butterflies, reluctant to disperse far from their favourite warm, south-facing hillsides. Males are aggressive and tenaciously defend their territories. They mate either on the ground, on tall grass stems or on flower-heads. Both sexes like to feed on nectar from common milkwort and hawkweeds, or marjoram in high summer, when they also fly with Adonis and Common Blues. Rock-rose is common on heathland and coastal sand dunes so the Brown Argus also colonizes these habitats, and here may sometimes fly with Silver-studded Blues. Since the markings of the female Silver-studded Blue are similar (see page 108) careful observation is required to distinguish between them.

Distribution: Confined to southern England and parts of the Welsh coastline, many colonies have disappeared because of agricultural disturbance. Coastal colonies exist in Cornwall, Devon and East Anglia, but most sites are on inland limestone and chalk downs, especially Salisbury Plain, the Cotswolds, the Chilterns and the North and South Downs. The butterfly is also found on the Isle of Wight and Anglesey, but nowhere north of Lincolnshire.

NORTHERN BROWN ARGUS
Aricia artaxerxes

Wingspan: 29 mm (♂ and ♀)   **Status:** R

Typical habitat: South-facing grassy slopes and hillsides
On the wing: June – July in a single brood
Adult: The Northern Brown Argus, with its dark brown upper wing-surfaces, is so similar to the Brown Argus that it used to be taken for a subspecies of that butterfly. In 1967, following genetic research, the Northern Brown Argus was finally recognized as a separate species. A distinguishing white spot occurs on the upper surface of the forewing, though in some colonies in northern England, this marking is absent. Both sexes are similarly marked, but the orange crescents on the forewing are larger on the female, and she is lighter brown. The wing undersides are brownish-grey with white spots, which frequently lack the black pupils of the Brown Argus.
Life cycle: Similar to the white, disc-like eggs of the Brown Argus, the Northern Brown Argus lays its eggs singly on the upper surface of rock-rose leaves, rather than on the underside. The eggs are easy to find in late June or, in northern parts of Scotland, in late July. Within a week they hatch and whilst small, the caterpillars feed on the underside of the leaves where they form distinct grooves. As they grow, ants attend them, attracted by their sugary secretion. Around September, after the second moult,

hibernation occurs low down in the leaf litter at the base of the foodplant. The following March, the larvae emerge, feeding exposed on the leaves. They reach full size after the fifth moult, when they are pale green with pink markings. The pupa is browny-green, with dark wing cases. Ants will probably bury it beneath the soil, but pupae have also been found covered with silken threads, deep in the leaf litter at the bottom of the foodplant. The pupa hatches within twenty-one days.

Observation and behaviour: This northern butterfly was one of the earliest to recolonize Britain after the last Ice Age, 10,000 years ago. Today it still lives in small isolated colonies of several hundred adults, on mountain and hillsides where glaciated debris is strewn. The presence of rock-rose determines the success of the colonies, although in certain areas, the larvae feed on common storksbill. The butterfly is difficult to approach because it always flies rapidly just above the ground in bright sunshine, occasionally stopping to feed on thyme or bird's-foot-trefoil. The males are territorial but stay in loose groups in the sheltered areas at the bottom of slopes, where they patrol for unmated females. Communal evening roosts occur, with adults perching head downwards on tall grasses and dead flower-heads.

Distribution: Apart from isolated colonies in the Peak District, Durham and the Lake District, the Northern Brown Argus is confined to Scotland, especially Perthshire, Angus and Aberdeenshire. The most northern colonies are in Sutherland, and scattered colonies in Dumfriesshire mark its southern Scottish range. Interestingly, the two Durham colonies still breed in the same localities as they did when originally discovered in 1827, illustrating the sedentary nature of this tiny butterfly.

COMMON BLUE
Polyommatus icarus

Wingspan: 35 mm (♂ and ♀)   **Status:** R

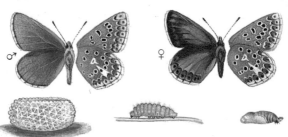

Typical habitat: Cliffs and undercliffs, downs, unimproved grassland, wasteland, heaths and disused quarries
On the wing: Mid-May – June and August – September in two distinct broods
Adult: This is the most common of the Blue butterflies; the male's bright, violet-blue upper wing-surfaces are well-known. Close observation reveals a white marginal fringe around all the wings, together with a thin black sub-marginal line. Throughout the range both sexes show great variety in colour, size and markings. The female is particularly variable in colour, ranging from brown upper wing-surfaces dusted with blue scales towards the body to purple-blue scales across all the surfaces. Both Irish and Scottish females are very blue. Females also show orange submarginal markings on all wings, whereas their wing undersides resemble those of the male, with black dots circled in white and with orange spots near the margins.
Life cycle: White, disc-shaped eggs are laid singly on the upper surface of terminal leaves of bird's-foot-trefoil, black medick, restharrow and clovers, depending on the habitat. Within nine days they hatch, and the green hairy caterpillars feed by day or night on the leaves, where they are surprisingly well-camouflaged. Like many caterpillars

of the Blues, their whereabouts may be revealed by the presence of ants. First-brood larvae found during June and July, are fully grown after the fourth moult and eventually pupate on the ground, where the green chrysalis is buried by ants. Second-brood larvae begin to feed in August but enter hibernation after their second moult, on a mat of silk attached to vegetation at the base of the foodplant. They continue to feed from April to May the following year.

Observation and behaviour: Constantly active in bright sunshine, Common Blues like to feed from vetches, trefoils and buttercups, though the second-generation brood prefer marjoram and thyme as a source of nectar. Both generations fly rapidly from flower to flower and perch with their wings held partially open. During dull weather and at roosting times, small groups may be found resting head downwards on stems of dead flowers or the seed-heads of tall grasses. Early each morning, they are still to be found in this position, waiting for the temperature to rise above 16°C, when they will disperse just above ground level. The butterfly is able to wander and colonize suitable new habitats. Between several dozen and a few hundred adults form the typical, discrete colony, which always tends to be a smaller group than that of other species of this family. The most favourable habitats have a mosaic of short and long turf, with bare patches of soil near the foodplant and the provision of sunlight and shelter.

Distribution: The Common Blue is no longer quite as common as its name suggests but is still found throughout the British Isles, with the exception of the highest uplands and the northern Shetlands. Modern farming methods and the associated destruction of its preferred grassland habitats are the chief threats to colonies of this butterfly throughout its range.

CHALKHILL BLUE
Lysandra coridon

Wingspan: 38 mm (♂ and ♀)

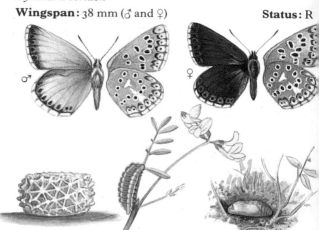

Typical habitat: Sunny open downlands, disused quarries and earthworks, and limestone hillsides

On the wing: July – August in a single brood. Occasionally a second brood is possible in favourable summers.

Adult: With their pale silvery-blue upper wings, Chalkhill Blue males are unmistakeable; when basking the black margins to the forewings can be clearly seen. The undersides of the wings are greyish with black spots surrounded by white haloes. Additional orange spots occur on the hindwings. Females are quite different, with brown upper wing-surfaces tinged with blue scales near the body. All the wings of the female have white fringes marked with brown, and inside this marginal fringe, pale-orange dots occur. Those on the hindwing show black pupils. The underside of the hindwing is brown, but otherwise all other markings are similar to those of the male.

Life cycle: Restricted mainly to south-facing chalk downs, the colonies of this butterfly are controlled by the availability of horseshoe vetch, the main larval foodplant. The single white eggs are laid on a stem or leaf as the female crawls around the plants. They are easy to find during August, but eventually drop to the ground where they hibernate through the winter. Upon hatching in March, the larvae remain largely on one plant of horseshoe vetch all their lives. They reach full size after the fourth moult. Green and yellow, they are similar to Adonis Blue caterpillars which live on the same foodplant. During the daytime the larvae rest at the base of the stems, feeding mainly at night. At all times they are attended by ants, seeking sugar secretions from their 'honey gland'. The chrysalis is pale green and because it also produces a sweet secretion it is buried and thus protected by ants, either just below the soil surface, or deep in surface vegetation. The butterfly emerges within a month.

Observation and behaviour: All colonies are discrete and the butterflies are largely sedentary, seeming reluctant to fly across separating valleys from one suitable site to another. Both sexes enjoy sunshine, frequently basking on the ground or on plants such as carline and stemless thistles, marjoram and eyebright, where they perch for nectar. Males, in particular, are often seen obtaining moisture from fox or rabbit droppings. They are gregarious, flying in groups whenever the temperatures are above 15°C. At dusk, communal roosts of Chalkhill Blues are common, clinging head downwards to the stems of grasses and dead flower-heads growing in sheltered positions at the foot of the hillsides.

Distribution: Typically, the Chalkhill Blue is a butterfly of the old calcareous grasslands found in southern Britain. Cambridge, the Chilterns and the Cotswolds mark the northern limit of its range. All colonies fluctuate annually. Many of the southern counties retain good colonies. The North and South Downs, Dorset coastline and the chalk hills of Kent, Sussex, Hampshire and Wiltshire all support colonies on their south-facing slopes, some of them in managed Nature Reserves.

ADONIS BLUE
Lysandra bellargus

Wingspan: 38 mm (♂ and ♀)　　　　　　　　**Status:** R

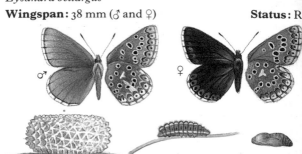

Typical habitat: Short-turf downland, especially south-facing, warm slopes

On the wing: Late May – June and August – September in two distinct broods

Adult: Brilliant turquoise-blue upper wing-surfaces distinguish the male Adonis Blue from any other species. White marginal fringes marked by the endings of black veins are equally diagnostic. Inside the white margins, a continuous black line runs around the perimeter of all the wings. The undersides are greyish, dotted with black spots bearing white haloes; the hindwing undersides also have a marginal row of orange spots. Females have chocolate-brown upper wing-surfaces, dusted with blue scales towards the body. Black and orange eyespots run around the edges of all the wings, just inside their white margins. Underside markings resemble those of the male, although the ground colour is browner, and the marginal orange spots occur on both wings.

Life cycle: Each June and September, the greeny-white eggs are laid singly on young leaves of horseshoe vetch. They hatch within twenty-two days. Depending on the season, the young larvae eat the leaves, flowers or fresh seed-pods by daylight. Fully grown, the green-and-yellow caterpillars are well-camouflaged on the foodplant and resemble larvae of the Chalkhill Blue, which also feed on horseshoe vetch. From the second instar onwards, the caterpillars are constantly fussed over by ants. Caterpillars of the first generation pupate at five weeks, whereas those of the second hibernate in October, at the base of the grass mat, and recommence feeding in late March. The pale-brown pupa is difficult to find, because it forms underground in cracks in the soil, or in the brood chambers of ants' nests. It hatches within three weeks.

Observation and behaviour: Horseshoe vetch is restricted to calcareous grassland, and of this terrain, the Adonis Blue prefers the warmest spots on hillsides where the turf is shorter than three centimetres and maintained by regular grazing. Females only choose plants in sunny hollows, preferring those growing in sheep ruts, in hoof prints or next to bare soil. Once suitable individual plants are found, as many as thirty eggs are deposited. The butterfly breeds in very discrete colonies, ranging in size from hundreds to many thousands, depending on the quality of the summer. All of the 150 known colonies fluctuate in size annually. The butterflies are reluctant to stray and colonize even the closest of suitable new sites. As a sun-worshipping species, they fly swiftly in warm weather, taking nectar from horseshoe vetch, stemless thistle and marjoram, but also obtaining moisture from bare soil patches or rabbit droppings. The males are non-territorial, but prefer the sheltered lower slopes and hillside hollows, where they mate with females, as soon as the latter emerge. Towards late afternoon and during unfavourable weather, the Adonis Blues roost on long grass stems, often in small groups.

Distribution: Britain is the northern limit of the Adonis Blues' European range, and the species is confined to a few downs in southern England. Half of the colonies are in Dorset, with others in Wiltshire, Surrey, Sussex, Kent and the Isle of Wight. A few localized colonies exist in Hampshire and Avon, with appearances having been noted in the Chilterns. Generally, however, the species is suffering a severe decline due to habitat destruction.

HOLLY BLUE
Celastrina argiolus

Wingspan: 35 mm (♂ and ♀)   **Status:** R

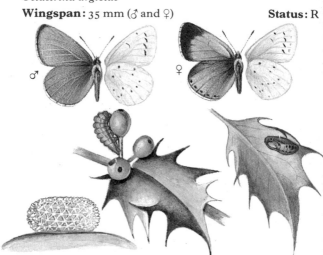

Typical habitat: Gardens, parks, hedgerows and woodlands

On the wing: April – May and July – August in two distinct broods

Adult: Although both sexes of the Holly Blue are the same shade of blue on the upper wing-surfaces, there are differences in markings. The male has narrow black borders at the margins of the lilac-blue wings, whereas the female has wider black borders on the costal and outer margins of all the wings. The wing undersides of both sexes are light-blue with black dots.

Life cycle: Most interestingly, the white, disc-shaped eggs of the spring brood are laid on holly, but those laid by the late-summer butterflies are deposited on ivy. Sometimes alternative foodplants, including dogwood and spindle, are used for egg-laying. The eggs are positioned at the base of the flower buds and hatch within a week. Resembling green slugs when fully grown, the caterpillars of the spring brood chew into the unripe holly berries, creating minute holes. Sometimes eggs are laid at the base of flower buds on male holly bushes; this is suicidal, because without developing berries, the caterpillars die. The August caterpillars feed on the ivy flower buds and developing berries, chewing grooves into them until only the stalks remain. They are so perfectly camouflaged that only an experienced eye will detect them. The illustration shows the green and rose-pink caterpillar which is slightly rarer than the usual yellowish-green form, but easier to see. After about six weeks, the brown pupa is formed, fixed by a silken girdle to the underside of a leaf, a crevice in the trunk of the shrub, or in leaf litter on the ground. Second-brood pupae overwinter, hatching the following April.

Observation and behaviour: Because of the larval foodplants it depends on, this Blue thrives in town parks and gardens where ornamental ivys and hollies are planted. Unlike other Blues, the Holly Blue is a fairly nomadic species, wandering from one area to another. Equally, however, self-contained colonies can remain on particular sites for many years. Drinking nectar from flowers is unusual for this butterfly, but in parks snowberry blossom is a favourite. At rest, the wings are held characteristically half-open, revealing both surfaces. Generally it prefers to feed on trees running sap from a wound, or on moisture from a damp patch of soil. Around mid-morning, females begin egg-laying activity, but only when the sun falls across the foodplant. They will fly in breezy conditions, but aerial and egg-laying activity ceases with a north-easterly wind. During courtship, the male lands beside a perched female and walks around her with wings partly open and his whole body vibrating, before mating.

Distribution: In southern England, the Holly Blue can be found wherever holly and ivy grow, although populations fluctuate mysteriously from year to year. The species is locally abundant in Wales, Cumbria, south-west Scotland and southern Ireland.

LARGE BLUE
Maculinea arion

Wingspan: 40 mm (♂), 43 mm (♀)

Status: R
(*reintroduced*)

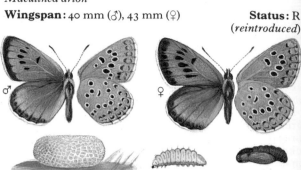

Typical habitat: Grassy hillsides where the turf is short

On the wing: July, in a single brood

Adult: The male has blue upper wing-surfaces marked with black spots and borders, whereas the undersides are grey-blue with black spots surrounded by white haloes. The wings have white fringes which are also present in the female, although the blue on her upper wing-surfaces is brighter and the black markings are deeper. Black spots and markings vary between individuals within a colony.

Life cycle: The Large Blue shows perhaps the most fascinating life cycle of all British butterflies. Lack of knowledge of its specific requirements was partly responsible for the butterfly's extinction in 1979. It needs short turf, grazed by rabbits, where up to sixty eggs may be laid on wild thyme. After about ten days the grey-white eggs hatch, and the young larvae feed on the seeds and flowers of thyme for between two and three weeks. Their pink bodies with white hairs, perfectly match the flower-heads. During the second instar, the caterpillar drops to the ground and within a few hours it will be discovered by the red ant (*Myrmica sabuleti*) which builds its nest on undisturbed, short-turf grassland. The caterpillar secretes a sweet solution from a special gland on its tenth segment which is attractive to the ant. Eventually the caterpillar is carried underground into the ants' nest, where it feeds on ant larvae for a further nine months. During this time, a single Large Blue caterpillar will eat about 400 ant larvae, so more than one caterpillar in a nest will destroy the ant colony, resulting in their own starvation. The pale-brown pupa forms below ground, inside an ant chamber, where it hatches after three or four weeks. The butterfly crawls out of the nest to the surface, where it rests between two and three hours, drying its wings.

Observation and behaviour: The Large Blue occurs throughout central and southern Europe, apart from regions of the Iberian Peninsula. In Britain most of the known breeding-sites were lost to the plough or conifer plantations and even in Europe its populations are declining. It is not a particularly fast-flying butterfly and prefers to travel only short distances from one flower to another. There is still much to be learnt about its secretive but fascinating life-cycle, but within the last fifteen years, scientists have at least learnt enough to breed this species in captivity and reintroduce the butterfly into managed habitats.

Distribution: In 1953, myxomatosis killed thousands of rabbits, which thus reduced the amount of grazing, so that the butterfly's specialized habitats became overgrown and the thyme shaded by scrub growth, causing its numbers to decline. The main localities of the Large Blue prior to 1979 were all in the West Country, where they formed discrete colonies. In 1983, similarly-marked Swedish stock was reintroduced to specially-prepared breeding sites at secret locations. Because of skilful management, this influx resulted in four generations of British colonists. Adults emerged from ants' nests in the summers of 1985 and 1986, and up to ten Large Blues flew across hillsides in the West Country. During 1987, the success continued, with more than seventy-five adults laying over 2,000 eggs. In 1988 150 adults produced 4,500 eggs and it seems likely that the Large Blue is here to stay.

DUKE OF BURGUNDY FRITILLARY
Hamearis lucina

Wingspan: 29 mm (♂), 32 mm (♀)   **Status:** R

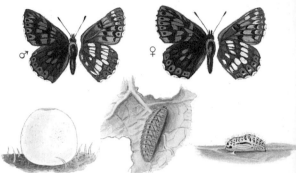

Typical habitat: Scrubby calcareous grassland and sheltered woodland rides and glades

On the wing: Mid-May – June in a single brood

Adult: Despite resembling a Fritillary, with its tawny-orange and brown-black upper wings, this butterfly belongs to the family *Nemeobiidae*, or Metalmarks. On the hindwing undersides, twin white bands distinguish the butterfly from any British Fritillary. The females have six walking legs, whereas males have only four.

Life cycle: Cowslip and primrose are the only two larval foodplants of this species, with cowslip being much preferred. The pale-yellow eggs are laid in groups of two to five on the underside of the leaves, and hatch within two weeks. They are easily found by the trained eye during June. Normally, small holes in the leaf surface draw attention to the feeding caterpillars, which rest on the undersurface in their earlier stages of growth. They become fully grown after the third moult and are extremely hairy, with pale-brown bodies. At this stage they leave the foodplant and hide in leaf litter during the day, returning to eat the leaves at night. The cream, black-spotted and striped pupa is of the girdled form, attached to the underside of the foodplant leaf. The larva hibernates through the winter, with the butterfly hatching the following May.

Observation and behaviour: The males are easiest to locate because they set up observation posts, overlooking their territory. Grass tussocks or overhanging twigs at the intersection of woodland rides or pathways are favourite sites, but other sun-spots amongst scrub vegetation are also popular. Any butterfly passing the look-out perch is vigorously pursued and intercepted, in case it is an unmated female, but after every flight, the male returns to the original perch. Unless removed by habitat destruction, these same perches are used by successive generations of males year after year, although the actual colonial breeding sites may vary slightly as foodplants become overshaded. The males are aggressive by nature, whereas females are shy. They are mated immediately after they emerge. Mating only takes place on calm days, usually in the mornings, whilst the insects are perched on low bushes or dead flower stems. Females then tend to ignore the male territories and lead a secluded existence, looking for ideal egg-laying sites. The largest leaves of primrose, partially shaded but not overgrown, are preferred. Traditional woodland sites have in recent years been deserted, in favour of scrubby downland areas where cowslips predominate. The Duke of Burgundy is a restless species, dashing throughout the habitat, feeding chiefly on honeydew, or sometimes the nectar of wood spurge, buttercup and hawthorn.

Distribution: Once found in Wales and southern Scotland, this species is now almost entirely confined to the woods and scrubland of southern England. Isolated populations occur around Morecambe Bay, Scarborough and Peterborough, but the butterfly's stronghold appears to be the scrubland valleys and woodland clearings of the Cotswolds. Only about 250 colonies remain; many are declining as the habitat becomes unsuitable, although some large colonies exist on maintained Nature Reserves.

WHITE ADMIRAL
Ladoga camilla

Wingspan: 60 mm (♂), 64 mm (♀)   **Status:** R

♀

Typical habitat: Large deciduous woods and margins of young conifer plantations

On the wing: July – early August in a single brood

Adult: Apart from the fact that the male is a slightly darker blackish-brown on the upper wing-surface, both sexes are similarly marked. The wing undersides are the most attractive surfaces, with orange-bronze predominating and black, white and blue-grey scales occurring near to the body.

Life cycle: The rounded, honeycombed and spiked eggs are laid singly on the upper margins of honeysuckle leaves, and hatch within a week. After eating their own eggshell, the larvae move to the leaf midribs near the tip. The caterpillars are easy to find, because of their characteristic feeding pattern. They nibble away the leaf, but allow the midrib to remain intact, and settle on it for camouflage. The second moult occurs in August, and hibernation begins in September. Using silken threads, the remainder of a leaf is pulled together, forming a tent. The caterpillar remains inside this hibernaculum until next April. When feeding resumes in the spring, the larva perches on stems of honeysuckle. It is bright green with russet spines. The hanging pupa is light green and attractively marked with silvery-metallic protrusions and purple-brown outlines, resembling a withered leaf.

Observation and behaviour: The White Admiral is an elusive species, preferring to remain out of sight high in the canopy, feeding on aphid honeydew. Both sexes are powerful, swift fliers and can be seen soaring and gliding against the sky, before tumbling back towards the upper branches. With their elegant, flitting movements, they are sometimes confused with the Purple Emperor, but are in reality much smaller, as can be seen when they descend to feed on bramble blossom. Males prefer to claim territories which capture the sunshine; conversely, egg-laying females use only thin, dangling strands of honeysuckle in partial shade. Here, up to 200 eggs are laid. If the temperatures in June are suitably high, then development takes place more quickly. Eighty per cent of all maturing larvae are eaten by birds and only one or two of all the eggs laid in a batch will ever complete the full life cycle to become an adult the following year.

Distribution: Found throughout central Europe, this species is confined to the woodlands of southern and eastern England, the northern limit of its breeding range. The strongholds are in Buckinghamshire, Oxfordshire, Berkshire, Wiltshire, Sussex, Surrey, Hampshire and Dorset, where the species remains locally abundant. The White Admiral is rare in East Anglia, and is localized around Peterborough, which represents its most northern site. It is isolated in south-west Wales.

PURPLE EMPEROR
Apatura iris

Wingspan: 75 mm (♂), 84 mm (♀)

Typical habitat: Large deciduous woods and forests
On the wing: July – August in a single brood
Adult: With similarly-shaped wings that have an overall, dusky-brown ground colour, white markings and a russet-ring on the hindwing, both sexes initially appear identical. However, when sunlight hits the wings of the male, they refract the light and turn an unforgettable, iridescent purple. The wing undersides of both sexes are similar.

Life cycle: The eggs, which are green at first, later acquire a purple band. They are dome-shaped and laid singly on the upper surface of willows. Hatching within two weeks, the caterpillar is greenish-yellow with a black head. After the first moult the yellow-brown horns appear on the caterpillar's head, with a similarly coloured saddle halfway down its body. At this stage it hibernates, attached to a silken pad in the fork of a twig, changing colour to match that of the branch. Feeding resumes in March and by May the larvae are fully-grown, green with yellow body markings. Inactive in the daytime, they feed at night, when they roam right across the bush, but always return to their silken pad before daylight. Suspended by tail hooks from a pad of silk, the chrysalis hangs under a willow leaf; being grey-green in colour, it is difficult to see.

Observation and behaviour: Both sexes group around the top of a particularly tall tree, called a 'master tree', where they court, mate and roost. Males are generally seen flying across the canopy of ash, oak and beech woods, where they patrol a territory which they fearlessly defend from their base in the master tree. Towards late afternoon they descend to drink moisture from puddles along tracks. Alternatively, they feed from animal carcasses, and fox, deer or rabbit droppings. Females are seldom seen. Courtship involves twisting, earthbound flights, as the female rejects the advances of her suitor. When ready to mate, she leads the male across the woodland canopy to a leafy platform. The females disperse to lay their eggs, usually between mid-day and two p.m. in sunny weather. They are particular where the eggs are placed, and only six to ten eggs may be deposited in shade during this time.

Distribution: This butterfly is now virtually confined to central southern England, especially the woods on the clay soils of Sussex and Surrey. Other colonies exist in Hampshire, Wiltshire, Nottinghamshire, Oxfordshire and Peterborough.

RED ADMIRAL
Vanessa atalanta

Wingspan: 67 mm (♂), 72 mm (♀)　　　　　　　**Status:** SM

Typical habitat: Almost anywhere, including parks, gardens, woods, hedgerows and orchards

On the wing: May – October in two possible broods

Adult: Because this butterfly, with its striking markings, is a frequent visitor to the garden buddleia, it is one of our best-known species. The sexes are similar, with black upperwings marked with red bands and white patches on the forewings. The underside of the forewings is a paler replica of the upper surface, but the hindwing undersides are brown, grey and black.

Life cycle: Females lay the oblong, ridged eggs singly on the upper surface of tender stinging-nettle leaves. As the embryo matures, it turns from light green to black before hatching in seven days. The young caterpillar immediately crawls to the leaf base and pulls the edges together with silk to form a tent-like structure. As it grows, the solitary caterpillar forms a tent from several leaves, which is easy to find, especially during July. Caterpillars are variably coloured and can be black with yellow patches on the side and yellow spines, or olive-grey with yellow or brown side-markings and black spines. The larval stage lasts a month before the chrysalis is formed, hanging from a silken pad inside the final larval tent. It is light grey marked with gold, and hatches within seventeen days.

Observation and behaviour: The Red Admiral is one of our main migrants, arriving from the Mediterranean in May. Sometimes it overwinters in Britain as a butterfly, sheltering in hollow trees, caves and buildings, but the majority of spring sightings are of migrants. The spring visitors mate and produce a second, summer brood. In autumn these adults feed on buddleia, michaelmas daisies and rotten fruit, and often bask with wings wide open. They also like to feed on sap from a wound on a tree, where they form groups. If disturbed, they take off in powerful flight, interspersed with wing-flicks and glides. Numbers arriving in the British Isles vary annually, according to European conditions. Successful breeding in the Mediterranean leads the butterflies to search for breeding areas and nectar elsewhere. Deserts to the south force the butterflies north to Britain, where the males quickly set up territories in habitats which are sheltered and attract the sun. As breeding finishes and late summer arrives, both sexes become absorbed in feeding, jostling alongside Peacocks and Small Tortoiseshells. They will fly well after sunset.

Distribution: Upon arrival, the Red Admiral disperses throughout the British Isles, including the offshore islands as far north as the Shetlands. The Scottish Highlands and all of Ireland are colonized. Throughout its range the butterfly is easily seen and recognized.

PAINTED LADY
Cynthia cardui

Wingspan: 64 mm (♂), 70 mm (♀)   Status: SM

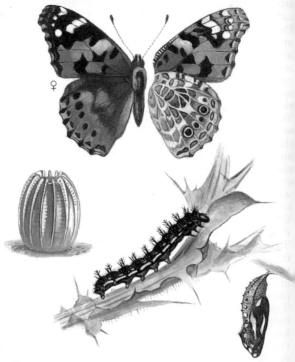

♀

Typical habitat: Gardens, woodland margins, rough grassland and verges

On the wing: Mid-May – June and August – September in two probable broods

Adult: As the Painted Lady frequently settles with open wings, the pale pinkish-orange, upper wing-surfaces, marked with black and white, are very familiar. The

132

underside of the forewing is a duller version of the upper surface, but the hindwing underside is particularly beautiful. Here patterns of blue, olive-green, grey and brown make the underside of this butterfly unique.

Life cycle: Thistles are the main larval foodplant of the Painted Lady, although nettles, burdocks and mallows are alternatives. The green eggs are distinctively keeled and, laid singly on the upper surfaces of the foodplant, are easily observed. They hatch within a week, and the small caterpillars crawl to the underside of the leaf, where they spin a silken shelter. Beginning on the outer, thin cuticle, the caterpillar eventually eats the whole leaf as it grows. When feeding on thistles, the spines are left. The larval webs and the larvae themselves are easy to find, especially during June and July when they are full size, black and spiny, with a yellow stripe down each side. After a month, the caterpillar moves from its feeding station and constructs a new silken tent, using foodplant leaves, in which it pupates. The pupa is grey with a pink tinge, marked with gold. It hatches within two weeks.

Observation and behaviour: Truly migratory, the Painted Lady can be found throughout the British Isles. Those adults reaching our shores in early summer began their life as eggs in North Africa. Following winter rains, the deserts of Africa rapidly bloom with a short-lived flush of vegetation. Here the caterpillars feed and rapidly pupate. As the butterflies emerge, the migration begins. The insects reach the Mediterranean by March, France by April and Britain by May, always seeking sun-trap habitats. Unable to survive our winters, the butterfly is on the wing until October. Males are territorial, occupying sun-spots on the ground where they bask, before making reconnaissance flights for unmated females. One or two generations are possible during an English summer.

Distribution: This species is to be found worldwide, including the Arctic Circle and Australia, but not South America. Although most common in southern Britain, it takes a large spring influx for the Painted Lady to disperse through the British Isles out to the smaller islands.

SMALL TORTOISESHELL
Aglais urticae

Wingspan: 50 mm (♂), 56 mm (♀)   **Status:** R

Typical habitat: Common everywhere, including parks, gardens and open countryside
On the wing: March – October in two distinct broods
Adult: Although the females are larger, both sexes are similarly marked. When basking, the orange-red ground colour of the open wings is very distinctive. Each forewing has six black patches and a single, white spot occurring towards the outer tips. The hindwings have a large black patch towards the body, which is frequently tinged with orange hairs. All four wings have dark margins containing bright-blue crescents. The underside of the wings is drab

and perfectly resembles a dead leaf. The tips of the antennae are pale yellow.

Life cycle: Between eight and nine raised ribs run from top to base of the pale yellowy-green, squat eggs. They are laid in batches of eighty to 200 on the underside of young terminal stinging-nettle leaves, growing in a sheltered position. The eggs hatch within twelve days. The small, gregarious caterpillars spin a white silken communal web around the leaves, dividing up into smaller groups of sixty to eighty as they grow. They reach full size at twenty-two millimetres, leaving the web to feed separately. Their variable yellow and black, spined bodies are easy to find before they disperse to pupate. The chrysalis is formed on vegetation or on walls, fences, and under the eaves of garden sheds. It is either dull brown or an attractive grey-pink, flushed with copper, and hatches after twelve days.

Observation and behaviour: Small Tortoiseshell butter-flies are highly mobile; within any one day an individual will fly a distance of nearly two kilometres (1.2 miles). They like to feed on the nectar of creeping thistle but are equally fond of buddleia and ice-plants growing in gardens. Hibernating in sheds, garages, coal bunkers or cool churches, the adults emerge in spring. The males take up territories close to the larval foodplant, where they bask, particularly during the morning and on small stones and bare soil which reflect the heat of the sun. Once a female is intercepted, mating takes place deep in the nettlebed, and is therefore difficult to see. In the south of England, two generations of the Small Tortoiseshell will fly, in the north only one. The southern spring brood is laid in May, and the summer eggs are laid during July. Adult male butterflies emerging in August make no attempt to bask and intercept females. Instead, both sexes spend most of their time feeding on nectar, storing food supplies ready for hibernation.

Distribution: Small Tortoiseshells are found throughout the British Isles, even on the highest mountains and remote Scottish islands, but their numbers fluctuate according to weather and the availability of nettles.

LARGE TORTOISESHELL
Nymphalis polychloros

Wingspan: 64 mm (♂), 70 mm (♀)　　　　**Status:** R

♀

Typical habitat: Woodland margins, verges and lanes near elm trees
On the wing: March – October in a single brood
Adult: Similar in appearance to the Small Tortoiseshell, both sexes of the Large Tortoiseshell are alike, with dull orange upper wing-surfaces marked with black and yellow.

The hindwings have blue marginal crescents, but unlike the Small Tortoiseshell, this butterfly has no blue markings on the upper forewing margins. The undersides are shaded brown and dark purple and are surprisingly hairy.

Life cycle: In spring, large batches of up to 200 eggs are laid in a tube encasing thin elm twigs. Each egg is conical, and their brown colour and position high in the canopy make them impossible to find. Sometimes eggs are laid on pear, cherry, sallow willow, birch, poplar or aspen trees, but wych elm and common elm are the most popular. After three weeks the eggs hatch and the larvae live on a silken communal web spun across the leaves. They become fully grown after the fourth moult and are black with orange lines, yellowish spines and white speckles. At this stage they each individually drop to the ground and pupate on a neighbouring shrub or tree, where they hang from a silken pad. An attractive pink-brown with gold spots, the pupae are difficult to find.

Observation and behaviour: In late summer the adult butterflies emerge and feed on a variety of flower nectar, including bramble, or on running sap from wounded trees. They hibernate in log piles, hollow trees or undisturbed buildings, where they remain until the following March. During spring Large Tortoiseshells take nectar from pussy willows. They absorb as much heat as possible by basking on the ground with wings fully open. The Large Tortoiseshell follows a nomadic lifestyle with no permanent colonies. The butterflies are constantly active, seldom perching.

Distribution: This is one of our rarest butterflies. Although it was once found across most of southern England, its appearances over the last few decades have been brief. Generally, summer observations are more frequent than spring sightings, but 1948 was the last year when this butterfly was commonly seen in either season. It is most likely to be seen in Wales and southern counties. Today, with the loss of elm trees through disease, its chances of being successfully re-established are slight.

PEACOCK
Inachis io

Wingspan: 63 mm (♂), 69 mm (♀)   **Status:** R

Typical habitat: Most types of countryside.
On the wing: March – October in a single brood. May be a partial second brood in September, in warm summers
Adult: The blue-black 'peacock eye' markings on the brown-red upper wing-surface are instantly recognisable. Both sexes have scalloped wing edges. The undersides are predominantly inky-black, offering camouflage.

Life cycle: Towards mid-May the pale-green eggs are laid in large batches of up to 500 on the underside of young, succulent stinging-nettle leaves. The egg-laying site is carefully selected by the female, who seeks both shelter and a controlled amount of mid-day sunshine to encourage the eggs' development. They hatch within two weeks. The young larvae then spin a communal silken web around the terminal nettle leaves, where they can be easily seen. Once they have exhausted the food supply, they move off together through the leaves to construct another leaf-web. After the fourth moult they reach full size and are velvety black, covered in white speckles and with black, forked spines. A typical hanging pupa, the yellowy-green chrysalis is marked with pink, grey and gold. It hangs beneath leaves, or from the stems of nettles, and hatches within two weeks.

Observation and behaviour: This beautifully-marked butterfly is typically nomadic. Despite being regular visitors to the garden where they feed on ice plant, buddleia and michaelmas daisies, they are most frequently seen close to woodland. When the butterflies emerge in July, they spend most of their time feeding on nectar, prior to hibernating in hollow trees, log piles and quiet buildings, which one generation will use after another. On warm days they awake and the males immediately claim territories along hedgerows and woodland margins. Intruding males are chased off, but wandering females are pursued at speed in an amazing courtship flight of spirals, twists and glides, before the butterflies alight to bask with wings wide open. Sometimes when the Peacock is disturbed at rest, it makes an audible 'hiss' by rapidly opening the wings, so that the forewing inner margin rubs against the hindwing costal margin. The eye spots and noise frequently deter predators.

Distribution: The Peacock is common throughout southern Britain, with the exception of upland Wales. Populations decrease northwards; concentrations do occur in west Scotland, but the butterfly is rare north of the Firth of Forth. Distribution occurs throughout Ireland.

CAMBERWELL BEAUTY
Nymphalis antiopa

Wingspan: 72 mm (♂), 84 mm (♀)   **Status:** RM

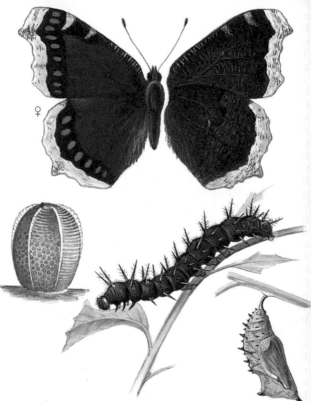

♀

Typical habitat: Scrubland, hillsides and clifftops in Britain; open woodland with nearby streams in Europe
On the wing: August – September
Adult: The Camberwell Beauty, with its dark-chocolate-

brown upperwings, creamy yellow margins and blue spots, is one of Britain's best-known species, though it never breeds there. The sexes are identically marked, and have dull brown wing undersides with an off-white margin.

Life cycle: The butterfly breeds throughout Europe, except in the Mediterranean islands and southern Spain. The red-brown eggs are laid in batches from thirty to over 200, on the twigs and branches of willows and birches. They hatch within twenty days, turning silvery-grey just before hatching. The larvae crawl away, spinning silk as they wander towards the tips of the branches. A communal web is spun around the leaves furthest from the trunk. After the fourth moult the caterpillar reaches full size and is black with a series of red dorsal markings. The entire body is covered with black spines bearing white hairs and there are numerous small, white warts which also bear fine hairs. Only when it is fully grown does the larva disperse away from the tree to pupate. The buff pupa, with black and orange patches, is difficult to see, hanging from its silken pad. Sharp, hard points cover the dorsal surface, replacing the larval spines. The entire body surface is covered in a white powder which gives the pupa a lilac bloom, similar to that found on plums. Within twenty-one days, it hatches.

Observation and behaviour: The butterfly's English name originates from the first specimen ever found, in Coldharbour Lane, Camberwell, in 1748. Although the butterfly has been known to hibernate and can therefore stand our winters, it has failed to breed. This is surprising, since all the larval foodplants occur commonly in Britain. It is rarely found near flowers, preferring to feed on trees running sap, especially silver birch. During autumn, rotting fruit in orchards is highly attractive.

Distribution: Common throughout Germany and Scandinavia, the powerful, direct flight of this migrant butterfly brings it to the south and east coasts of Britain from August onwards. Regular sightings have been reported in Scotland.

COMMA
Polygonia c-album

Wingspan: 55 mm (♂), 60 mm (♀)   **Status:** R

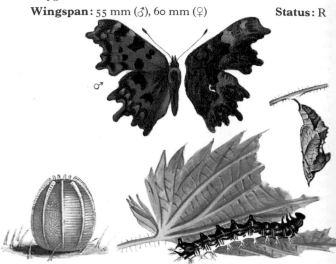

Typical habitat: Woodland rides and clearings, mature hedgerows and garden and scrubby hillsides
On the wing: March – October in two distinct broods
Adult: The jagged, irregular shape of the wing margins is unique to the Comma, which resembles a dead leaf when its wings are closed. The female is darker on the underside and has less jagged wing margins, but otherwise the sexes are similar. The wing uppersides are a rich orange, with brown and black markings, while the undersides are a mixture of brown and greeny-bronze with the white 'comma' that gives the species its name in the centre of the hindwing. Some of the Commas emerging in July have much paler markings and upper wing-surfaces of a bright fiery gold. In flight these individuals, of the form *hutchinsoni*, can be mistaken for Fritillaries.

Life cycle: The round, green eggs with clear white ridges are laid singly, or in twos or threes on the margins of nettle, hop or elm. Usually the upper leaf surface is selected. Whenever nettle is chosen, it is nearly always growing along the margins of woods or hedgerows. Within seventeen days the eggs hatch, and the greeny-buff caterpillar crawls beneath the leaf. After the first moult it turns brown with white patches and perfectly resembles a bird-dropping, which offers it excellent protection. Full size is reached after the fourth moult, when the caterpillar is tan brown with spines and a white dorsal patch. Orange and yellow markings cover the body. The pupa is formed within seven weeks and is suspended from a silk pad on the foodplant or neighbouring vegetation. The exterior is beautiful, with a pink-brown ground colour covered in gold and silver markings, but it is still hard to locate.

Observation and behaviour: Although typically a woodland butterfly, the Comma colonizes many other habitats and regularly visits the garden to feed on buddleia in late summer and rotting fruit in autumn. It is a strong and rapid flier, and males patrol woodland rides with tenacity, settling on a favourite perch overlooking their territory. Rival males are chased off, but females are courted to encourage them to mate. On most occasions, the male returns to the same observation twig or branch to continue watching over his occupied territory. Adults emerging from pupae in mid-summer generally breed the following year and spend their time greedily feeding on nectar from garden and park flower borders. Hibernation occurs with the onset of the first cold days and takes place in hollow trees, dense bramble or ivy. Commas hibernate until spring, emerging before the Small Tortoiseshells.

Distribution: During the last 200 years, the distribution of this butterfly has changed considerably. At the beginning of the twentieth century its range was restricted to the Wye Valley, but now it colonizes all of England south of York. No records have been noted of sightings in Scotland or Ireland, but it is locally common in lowland Wales. It is never found on high ground.

SMALL PEARL-BORDERED FRITILLARY
Boloria selene

Wingspan: 41 mm (♂), 44 mm (♀)   **Status:** R

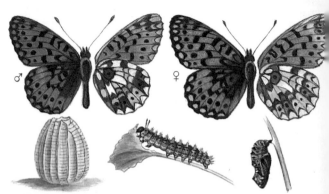

Typical habitat: Woodland clearings, grassy hillsides, moorland and sea cliffs

On the wing: June – mid-July

Adult: Although slightly smaller than the Pearl-bordered Fritillary, this species is very similar to the larger butterfly. Its black markings are of the same pattern but bolder, the upper wing-surfaces are a more vibrant orange-brown, and there are more white cells on the hindwing underside (between six and eight, as opposed to the two cells of the Pearl-bordered Fritillary). The wing undersides are bordered by silvery-white crescents.

Life cycle: Like the Pearl-bordered Fritillary, the ridged egg is laid on violets during June and July, or dropped near them. It turns grey with age. Both the dog violet and marsh violet are used for egg-laying, with the latter plant being the favourite in northern Britain. Within ten days the eggs hatch and the eggshell is eaten by the caterpillars. They are olive green, with dark spines. After the third moult, they hibernate in the dead undergrowth or inside curled leaves, until March, when they resume feeding.

Unlike those of the larger species, caterpillars of the Small Pearl-bordered Fritillary do not bask on the leaf surface, but remain well-hidden. Although they are daytime feeders, they only emerge briefly to chew the violet leaves, before rapidly descending again into the centre of the plant. After the fourth moult, they are fully grown. Their dark-brown bodies and paler spines are completely different from those of the Pearl-bordered Fritillary larvae. Marvellously camouflaged in the vegetation, the dark-brown pupa hangs from a silken pad and hatches within fourteen days.

Observation and behaviour: This species emerges a little later than the Pearl-bordered Fritillary, but there are several weeks in June when their flight periods overlap, and they may fly together in the same habitat. Freshly emerged and more vivid in colour, the Small Pearl-bordered Fritillary is the brighter of the two. It naturally prefers damper, more shaded conditions than its larger relative and is therefore more able to survive in an overgrown wood. It is less specific in its habitat colonization and is to be found on open moors close to violets, in Scotland and Cornwall, and on newly-established conifer plantations elsewhere. Several hundred adults form the isolated colonies. In sunny weather the males fly swiftly, barely above the ground, diving to feed on bugle or heather or to accost females. Where ground cover is sparse, the elusive females may be found, fluttering and perching on violet clumps to deposit eggs, in between feeding.

Distribution: Despite habitat destruction and change throughout this butterfly's range, it still remains reasonably common in western Britain, although it is absent from Ireland. In western Scotland it is common, becoming rarer in the south-east and not to be found in Caithness. Apart from Cumbria, lowland Wales, Devon and Cornwall, where the Fritillary remains locally common, it has declined everywhere else in England. In counties such as Dorset, Hampshire and Surrey, it is very localized. Only scattered colonies remain in the Midlands while fragmented but large colonies still exist in eastern England.

PEARL-BORDERED FRITILLARY
Boloria euphrosyne

Wingspan: 44 mm (♂), 47 mm (♀) **Status:** R

Typical habitat: Open woodland, especially rides and glades

On the wing: May – mid-June, normally in a single brood

Adult: Both sexes of this species have orange-brown upper wing-surfaces, marked with black veins, bars and spots, but the females are yellower than the males. The hindwing underside has two silver-white cells close to the body, which help in identification. The similarly-marked Small Pearl-bordered Fritillary has between six and eight of these white cells on the hindwing, in addition to the silver-white crescents along the margin which are common to both species.

Life cycle: When the finely-ridged, conical eggs are first laid in June, they are yellow, but they darken with age. Deposited individually, or sometimes in pairs, they are laid on or near a variety of violets. They hatch within two weeks. At first the larvae are straw-coloured with a jet-black head. After the first moult, the body hairs become black and spiny; hibernation takes place after the third moult. The caterpillars are hard to find at this stage, low down in dead undergrowth. They recommence day-time feeding the following March. After the fourth moult they are full-grown, and have dorsal spines with distinctive yellow bases. Because of its grey-brown coloration, the pupa resembles a dead, shrivelled violet leaf, and as it hangs suspended near the foodplant it is difficult to find. The butterfly emerges within ten days.

Observation and behaviour: This is the first Fritillary to be seen each year, gliding and flitting across woodland clearings in May and early June. Usually, colonies comprising several hundred adults may be found wherever trees have been felled; when coppicing was the standard form of woodland management, this species was abundant. Today, breeding occurs where deciduous trees have been replaced with conifers, but only for the first ten years of woodland growth, after which the shade is too dense for the species to survive. Both sexes like to feed on primrose and bugle nectar, resting or perching with wings closed. As late afternoon approaches, the Fritillary basks with open wings, preferably on bare patches of soil. Males emerge first each spring, actively patrolling up and down the clearings with occasional ground-level glides. They are searching for newly-emerged females and often attempt to mate with them before their wings are fully dry. Sometimes females are found on the ground amongst vegetation, rapidly vibrating their forewings; a signal, either of rejection or attraction, to soliciting males.

Distribution: Before 1950 this species was common in most dry woods in southern England and throughout Wales. Today it is largely absent from eastern England, with isolated populations in Sussex, Surrey, Kent and Yorkshire. Extinction threatens in the Midlands and in Oxford, Hampshire and Dorset it is very localized. South-west England, Wales and the Lake District remain the butterfly's stronghold, and it is relatively common here in open woods and on gorse-strewn coastal grassland. It is extremely localized in Scotland but common in the limestone area of the Burren in County Clare, Ireland.

QUEEN OF SPAIN FRITILLARY
Argynnis lathonia

Wingspan: 46 mm (♂), 54 mm (♀)   **Status:** RM

Typical habitat: Usually restricted to clifftops and open downland in southern England

On the wing: May – September

Adult: This rare migrant to Britain is extremely beautiful. It has a characteristic wing shape: the forewings are purposefully curved on their costal margins, whereas their outer margins are concave. Similar in its upper wing-markings to the Silver-washed Fritillary, the ground colour is a rich orange-brown, with black spots. All the wings show a lighter black marginal line on their upper surface. The presence of numerous large, silver patches on the underside of the hind wings distinguishes this species from all other Fritillaries.

Life cycle: Common in southern Europe, the Queen of Spain Fritillary rarely breeds in Britain. It cannot survive our winters, but occasionally the ribbed and conical eggs are laid on leaves and stems of common dog violet or sweet violet, to produce a brood of butterflies in August. The eggs are lemon-yellow when first laid, but they gradually darken and gain a grey-green tinge. Despite preferring to feed in bright sunshine, the caterpillars favour the shade and protection of the underside of the leaves when resting. They can be easily seen by the experienced observer in this position. After the fourth moult they are fully grown, slightly tapered at both ends. Their black bodies are covered with six rows of black, bristle-bearing spines, some of which have dark-red bases. After around twenty-three days, depending on weather conditions, the caterpillars pupate, hanging from a silken pad by their tail claspers. The pupa is brown, with black-and-white markings and an overall sheen. There may be two or three broods in a year, especially in southern Europe.

Observation and behaviour: The Queen of Spain Fritillary is on the wing from March to October throughout southern Europe, with migrants arriving in central Europe and Britain from May onwards. August and September are the usual months for observation in Britain, when the butterflies fly rapidly and powerfully across clifftops and grassland slopes. Sometimes this Fritillary shows a jerky, restless flight, similar to that of the Wall Brown. It cannot resist flowers (clovers provide the favourite source of nectar), and will also alight to feed on thistles, knapweeds and scabious wherever they grow. In bright sunlight, the silver patches on the wing underside are highly reflective and the butterfly appears to shimmer and flicker whilst in flight.

Distribution: North Africa and Mediterranean Europe are the main haunts of this butterfly, but its northerly migration takes it as far as southern Scandinavia. Each year, several sightings occur in Britain, most frequently in the southern and eastern counties of England, such as Norfolk, Kent, Sussex and Surrey, on downland and heaths. In Europe the butterfly colonizes dry hillsides up to 2,500 metres, open heath and grassland.

HIGH BROWN FRITILLARY
Argynnis adippe

Wingspan: 60 mm (♂), 67 mm (♀)　　　　**Status:** R

Typical habitat: Woodland clearings and margins, rough grassland and hillsides

On the wing: Late June – early August in a single brood

Adult: Males are bright orange-brown on the wing uppersides, with well-defined black lines and spots. Females are yellower and their wings are rounder in outline. The hindwing undersides of both sexes show a greenish tinge, and they are distinguished from the Dark-green Fritillary by a row of red dots near the margins, with silver pupils.

Life cycle: The ridged and keeled eggs are individually laid on, or near, sweet violet or common dog violet and are surprisingly difficult to find. This Fritillary overwinters in the egg stage. The eggs turn from pink to grey during the winter months, hatching around February. In its first instar, the caterpillar feeds on young violet leaves and flower buds; as it grows, it roams from plant to plant. By nature it is solitary, hiding low in the dead leaves, actively feeding during warm weather and reaching full size within three months. There are two colour forms: the dark variety is brown with white stripes and pinkish spines, whereas the light variety is reddy-brown with white stripes and reddish spines. The shiny, brown pupa is suspended from a silken pad under a leaf or deep in vegetation. It resembles a dead leaf and is difficult to find, despite rows of metallic gold spots along the dorsal surface. Within four weeks the pupa hatches.

Observation and behaviour: There is still much to be learnt about this secretive butterfly. It can be seen soaring over the woodland canopy, rapidly descending to feed on nectar from bramble and various thistles, when it is best approached. During adverse weather and at night, the High Brown Fritillary prefers to roost in the treetops. During warm, sunny weather it is particularly active, but individuals rarely stray from their isolated breeding colony.

Distribution: Little over thirty years ago, this Fritillary was well-distributed throughout England and Wales, but it is now a rare butterfly and absent from Scotland and Ireland. Throughout its range, populations are still declining, because the favourite woodland habitats are no longer managed by coppice rotation, and have simply become too overgrown and shaded. Even non-woodland colonies in western England are declining, but these remain the more productive of the two habitats. The insect's northern limit is around the Lake District, where some of the largest colonies remain, and it is still locally common in Wales. The Wyre Forest contains one of the largest woodland colonies and the numerous woods along the southern margin of Dartmoor and Exmoor afford regular sightings. In eastern England the butterfly is virtually extinct, although reports occur of populations in east Sussex, but nowhere does the distribution of this species give encouraging prospects for its long-term future.

DARK-GREEN FRITILLARY
Argynnis aglaja

Wingspan: 63 mm (♂), 69 mm (♀)   **Status:** R

Typical habitat: Rough, unfertilized grassland, sea cliffs, dunes, moors and heaths

On the wing: July – August in a single brood

Adult: Sometimes this Fritillary is confused with the High Brown Fritillary, because their habitats overlap and they fly together. The upper wing-surfaces are orange-brown with black spots, and the undersides are greenish-orange. This distinguishes the Dark-green Fritillary from the Silver-washed Fritillary, another similarly sized and marked butterfly. Running along the outer edge on the underside of the forewings is a sequence of characteristic silver spots. This is one of the best distinguishing features of the butterfly, absent from the High Brown Fritillary.

Of the three Fritillaries mentioned above, the Dark-green Fritillary is the most widely distributed. It varies in colour throughout its range. On Orkney and other northern islands, it is darker but smaller, whereas in Ireland the upper wings are red-brown. In certain Scottish localities a separate subspecies occurs, called *scotica*, which is not only larger than the typical form but more positively marked. The wing undersides of this subspecies are much greener, with distinctive silver patches.

Life cycle: The conical-shaped and ridged eggs are yellow when first laid, but acquire purple marks as they age. They are laid singly during July and August on the leaves and stems of hairy, marsh or common dog violets, growing in large patches, or on neighbouring plants. The type of violet favoured varies according to locality, but preferred sites are those patches growing in turf no taller than fifteen centimetres and lightly grazed by rabbits. The female butterfly crawls well inside the violet clump to lay her eggs, which hatch within eighteen days. Upon emerging, the pale-yellow caterpillar eats its eggshell before entering hibernation. The following spring, still in its first instar, it feeds on violet leaves, moving from one plant to another in diffused sunshine. The tips, margins and lobes of the leaves are all chewed, and this leaf damage is so obvious it acts as the best method of locating the fully grown purple-black larva, marked with red spots and white specks. Well-concealed in a loosely spun, tent-like cocoon, the chrysalis is formed deep in grass tussocks and violet clumps. The abdomen is dark brown, whereas the wings, head and thorax are black.

Observation and behaviour: Although its habitat is often windswept, the Dark-green Fritillary is a swift and powerful flier. Flying alone, it frequently stops to feed on nectar from thistles, common knapweed and field scabious. At sunset, it roosts in neighbouring tall grasses. Dark-green Fritillaries are difficult butterflies to get close to, but they are spectacular to watch as they pass at full speed, the males sometimes chasing the females.

Distribution: The greatest populations of this butterfly occur in coastal Scotland, Wales, Ireland and southern England. Numbers have drastically declined during the last fifty years, and in parts of Somerset and Devon they are now alarmingly scarce. Rough grassland in south-west England is still one of their strongholds.

SILVER-WASHED FRITILLARY
Argynnis paphia

Wingspan: 72 mm (♂), 76 mm (♀)　　　　**Status:** R

Typical habitat: Woodland rides and clearings, also some lanes and hedgerows

On the wing: July – August in a single brood

Adult: Although this is the last Fritillary to emerge each year, it is well worth waiting for, because it is the largest of the family. The sexes differ in colour, with the female being duller than the bright, orange-brown male. Females also lack the distinctive four black scent cells in the middle of the forewings, but all other black markings are similar to the males. The hindwing undersides of both sexes are a beautiful green, marked with four silvery bands. In the New Forest, and occasionally elsewhere, a form of Silver-washed Fritillary called *valezina* is found. The females of this subspecies have a distinctive green haze on their upper wing-surfaces and light pink on their forewing undersides.

Life cycle: Flying just above ground level, the female searches for patches of common dog violet. If she finds this plant, she selects a nearby tree and lays individual eggs in crevices in the bark, about two metres above the ground. Partially-shaded trunks with some moss growth are preferred and an ideally-located tree may accommodate as many as fifty eggs. The eggs are vertically ridged. They are laid during July and hatch within a fortnight. Emerging from the eggs, the caterpillars crawl deep into a crevice and hibernate; the following spring they descend the trunk in search of violets on the woodland floor. They are best discovered in late May when they are fully grown, dark brown with two yellow dorsal stripes and covered in dark-red spines. The caterpillars feed during the day and are active in sunshine, when they may be seen basking on leaves or eating the lobes. Pupae are difficult to find, because with their brown-and-gold markings, they resemble a dead leaf. They are attached to a silken pad, deep in ground vegetation.

Observation and behaviour: Like many Fritillaries, this species is a strong but graceful flier. Roosting takes place in the upper branches of trees and one of the butterflies' favourite pursuits is drinking the honeydew secreted by aphids feeding on the leaves. Males are especially alert when patrolling woodland rides, diving down to examine any brown leaf, in case it is a female or a rival male Fritillary. The courtship is exciting to watch: Silver-washed Fritillaries perform a tumbling, 'loop the loop' display flight, generally along a woodland ride. The compact breeding colonies are affected by weather conditions, because severe winters kill hibernating larvae and if the summers are wet with low temperatures, egg-bearing females refuse to deposit their eggs.

Distribution: The West Country remains a stronghold of the Silver-washed Fritillary, which colonizes woods and lanes in Cornwall, Devon and Somerset. Populations are maintained in Wales and Ireland but east of Hampshire and the West Midlands the butterfly is scarce, and it is virtually extinct in Kent and East Anglia.

MARSH FRITILLARY
Eurodryas aurinia

Wingspan: 42 mm (♂), 48 mm (♀)   **Status:** R

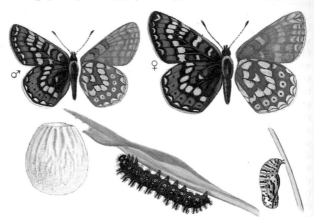

Typical habitat: Damp fields, moorland and grassland with plenty of shelter

On the wing: Late May – June in a single brood

Adult: Although the upper wing-surfaces are reddish-brown with black markings and yellow patches, this species does not share the typical patterns of other Fritillaries. The wing undersides are similar to the upper surfaces, but duller, and this is the only Fritillary with a single row of black dots near the margin of the hindwings. Colour and pattern variations are frequent. The females have rounder wings.

Life cycle: Soon after emerging the females mate, and then fly laboriously off to lay large batches of oval, ridged eggs on the underside of the leaves of devil's-bit scabious. The young larvae spin a communal web in which they feed and sunbathe in a conspicuous black mass. During September, they start to hibernate in a web deep in the vegetation, and recommence feeding in March. They stay together until the fifth instar, when each caterpillar wanders away. They become full-grown in the sixth instar, during May. Covered with bristles, they are totally black, with white, dust-like speckles on their sides. The chrysalis is difficult to find, since it is buff, marked with black and orange, and is suspended deep in the ground vegetation.

Observation and behaviour: Both sexes are noticeably weak fliers, fluttering and gliding to the nearest resting spot and requiring protection from the wind by scrub or tall vegetation. Males, which emerge first, fly more strongly, but immediately find somewhere to perch and rest. Both sexes, however, will fly to thistles, buttercups and tormentil for nectar. Colonies are only found where devil's-bit scabious grows in large patches and has developed mature leaves necessary to support larval food webs. The south- and west-facing slopes of short-turf downland are colonized, but again the foodplant needs to be readily available and the habitat lightly grazed by sheep or rabbits, if the colonies are to survive. Normally this species remains in isolated colonies and is very sedentary, but dispersal can occur in extremely warm summers, such as those of 1976 and 1983, when new sites were colonized. Larval populations are controlled by at least two parasitic wasps, while weather conditions are mainly responsible for breeding success. Sometimes the females, which lay between 300 and 500 eggs at a time, are so heavy with eggs that they are only able to take off in the warmest of conditions, and can be seen crawling around scabious.

Distribution: At one time this Fritillary was found throughout the British Isles in marshy fields, bogs and downland. Today habitat loss has led to its disappearance from many sites in eastern and southern England and the Midlands. Only isolated and declining colonies survive east of an imaginary line from Birmingham to Southampton, mainly on reserves or military land. Wiltshire, Hampshire, Dorset, Worcestershire and Cumbria remain the Marsh Fritillary's strongholds, although colonies still exist locally in Wales and west Scotland.

GLANVILLE FRITILLARY
Melitaea cinxia

Wingspan: 41 mm (♂), 47 mm (♀)   **Status:** R

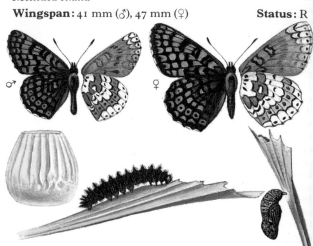

Typical habitat: Unstable, coastal cliffs and sheltered uncultivated slopes facing south

On the wing: June – early July in a single brood

Adult: Both sexes of the Glanville Fritillary are similar, with orange-brown upper wing-surfaces, marked with black, although the amount of black varies. Along the trailing upper edges of both hindwings are orange circles with black pupils. The underside of these wings are cream with two orange bands. The body of the female is fatter than that of the male and her wings are more rounded.

Life cycle: During June and July the oval, yellow eggs are laid in variable batches from fifty to 200 on ribwort plantain, or sometimes buck's-horn plantain. They are deposited on the underside of the leaves and hatch within three weeks. It seems that the female must find shelter and warmth for the eggs to be laid because exposed north-facing slopes are rarely colonized. Bare ground, in which land slips have created hollows, appears to be favoured, once plantain has taken hold. Living gregariously in silken webs spun over the foodplant, the caterpillars are easily found. Some webs contain hundreds of the black larvae with red-brown heads and black body spines. As late summer arrives, the caterpillars spin a hibernating web some distance from the foodplant, often in taller grasses, where they remain until the following February. In spring the webs are discarded but the larvae remain in groups, swarming across the foodplant to feed in sunshine. They remain concealed in the grass during overcast weather. The size of the larval colonies is determined by the availability of the correct plantains, because the caterpillars gorge themselves on the leaves, frequently stripping plants bare. Eventually each caterpillar wanders away and forms a grey, black and orange pupa in dense undergrowth. The butterfly emerges within three weeks. Since plantain, the larval foodplant, generally only colonizes newly-disturbed, unshaded ground, continuous land slippage and erosion are needed if new sites are to be formed and the butterfly is to survive.

Observation and behaviour: The easiest way to get close to the Glanville Fritillary is when it is feeding on nectar from bird's-foot-trefoil, thrift and clovers. At all other times, its flight is low and fast, frequently interspersed with floating glides. This low-level flight technique probably protects the butterfly from being swept over the cliffs on rising thermals. Males may be seen patrolling regularly, often in large numbers, hugging the low contours and coombes of undercliffs. Females stray on to the cliff tops, where they search for egg-laying sites.

Distribution: Found throughout Europe, except parts of Spain and Scandinavia, Britain represents the northern limit of this butterfly's range. It is only found on the Channel Islands and the Isle of Wight, where it is confined to the south coast, especially the sandstone cliffs. The majority of the breeding colonies are on National Trust property, where they are protected and managed, but still only half of the colonies are healthy in number.

HEATH FRITILLARY
Mellicta athalia

Wingspan: 40 mm (♂), 44 mm (♀)   **Status:** R

Typical habitat: New woodland clearings, young forestry plantations and some heaths

On the wing: Late June – July in a single brood

Adult: Apart from the fact that the males are darker, both sexes of the Heath Fritillary are similarly marked, with the upper wings typical of the Fritillary family. There are no brown spots on the wing undersides and this makes the Heath Fritillary unique, although the cream, orange and black markings are similar to those of the other Fritillaries.

Life cycle: The pale-yellow, conical eggs are laid in large batches, with sometimes up to 150 in a single batch, under leaves of bramble and other vegetation near the caterpillar's foodplants. They are well-concealed. The small, black, bristly larvae, which hatch within two weeks, crawl to one of these foodplants and spin a web in which they live and feed. The observer will find that in Kent, the larvae feed on common cow-wheat growing in open woodland. In Cornwall, cow-wheat may be eaten on one site, but elsewhere in the same county, ribwort plantain will be the favourite larval foodplant. Other south-western sites support young larvae on germander speedwell. During May the larvae become full-grown and are easy to find when they bask in groups on dead leaves. The suspended pupa is white and attractively marked with orange and black, but it is difficult to find, deep in dead leaves and ground vegetation.

Observation and behaviour: Like all other Fritillaries, this is a conspicuous butterfly, but it is very rare. It lives in isolated colonies in open sheltered woodland. Its flight is slow, with frequent glides, and it prefers to bask or drink nectar from bugle or thistles. Females are secretive by nature but males may be observed weakly patrolling up and down rides and clearings. This poor aerial ability probably prevents the Heath Fritillary from dispersing to colonize any new suitable habitats. Any new site therefore must be close to an already-existing, discrete colony. As woodland clearings become overgrown, so the populations of several thousand butterflies will gradually decline and eventually disappear. However, this is one species which may benefit from the effects of the hurricane in October 1987, which naturally created clearings in several Kent sites.

Distribution: This butterfly is found throughout Europe apart from Corsica and Sardinia, but it has always been very localized in Britain and confined to Essex, Kent, Sussex, Somerset, Devon and Cornwall. During the last seventy years its distribution has contracted further as coppice woodland-management has declined, and today the Heath Fritillary is probably the rarest resident butterfly under greatest threat of extinction. In 1980 a survey revealed that it was restricted to about five woods in the West Country, and three sites within Blean Wood near Canterbury, where it is slightly more numerous. The species is strictly protected by the 1981 Wildlife and Countryside Act and all of its remaining sites are now managed, to provide ideal breeding conditions. Some are official Nature Reserves. Only with such protection of both habitat and butterfly will this species be saved.

SPECKLED WOOD
Pararge aegeria

Wingspan: 47 mm (♂), 50 mm (♀)　　　　**Status:** R

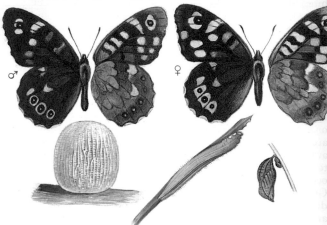

Typical habitat: Shady woodlands, but also hedgerows, country lanes and scrubland

On the wing: March – October in a succession of broods

Adult: Both sexes have pale-yellow patches on all wings, contrasting with the dark-brown background colour. The yellow patches are smaller and less distinct in the male, but both sexes have three black eyes with white pupils on the hindwings, and a single identical eye-spot towards the apex of the forewings. The butterfly resembles a dead leaf when its wings are closed, for the wing undersides are intricately marked in diffused grey and brown.

Life cycle: The translucent, yellow-green eggs are laid individually on the blades of grasses shaded by shrubs, and are difficult to locate. Hatching after ten days, the pale-green caterpillars with darker green, yellow and white stripes, are also elusive. They are characterized by their paired posterior 'tails' which are white, covered with grey hairs. The variably coloured chrysalis is suspended from a grass stem or blade, and is either pale green or yellowish-brown. Either the caterpillar or chrysalis may hibernate; autumn chrysalises produce butterflies the following spring, whereas butterflies emerge from the summer chrysalises within a month.

Observation and behaviour: The butterfly favours shady, damp habitats, in which its wing markings blend with the dappled sunlight during its dancing, fluttering flight. It may be confused with the Wall or Meadow Brown in flight. The males like to bask with open wings in vigorously defended sunspots, where sunlight lances through the tree canopy on to bramble leaves and blossom or a mossy bank. Females passing through the sunspots are pursued and rapidly courted, but trespassing males are chased off in a 'dog-fight', which spirals upwards towards the leaf canopy and only finishes when the occupying male has successfully defended his territory. Other battles occur when the butterflies descend after drinking honeydew in the canopy and hustle with Ringlets and Meadow Browns around bramble blossom.

Distribution: After the range declined greatly in the nineteenth century, populations have increased during the last forty years throughout England, south of Liverpool and the Humber, and in Wales and Ireland. The 1976 drought checked the population, because the Speckled Wood favours dampness and shade, but recolonization has occurred. In East Anglia and Scotland, where the butterfly is localized, its range is expanding.

WALL BROWN
Lasiommata megera

Wingspan: 44 mm (♂), 48 mm (♀)   **Status:** R

Typical habitat: Hedgerows, rough grassland and verges and woodland margins

On the wing: May – mid-June and August – early September

Adult: The ground colour of the Wall Brown's wings is orange-brown, with black-brown borders, veins and wavy lines, which are much bolder in the male. Females lack the dark band of scent scales crossing diagonally across the males' forewings, but both sexes have a series of pupilled eyespots on their wings. The underside of the hindwings is delicately marked with grey and brown patterns, which camouflage the butterflies perfectly when they are perched with closed wings.

Life cycle: Immediately after being laid on grass blades and exposed rootlets, the spherical eggs are green, but they turn white within days. Then they are easier to find along path edges or rabbit scrapes. The first-brood caterpillars are nocturnal feeders, and are difficult to find on the sheltered grass blades they prefer, but their green bodies, with a bluish tinge and white stripes, are quite distinguishable. After thirty-five days they reach full size, and hang among the grasses to form the green-and-yellow marked chrysalis, defying detection. Second-brood caterpillars overwinter, feeding during daylight whenever the mild weather allows them and remaining as larvae for nearly eight months.

Observation and behaviour: As its name suggests, this butterfly likes to bask with open wings on a wall, a patch of sunlit, bare ground, or a tree trunk, but males also like to perch and patrol. Perching occurs at the beginning and end of the day. Once warmed by the sun, males actively patrol for females, around mid-day. Their tawny colour makes them easily confused with aerial Commas and Fritillaries. If disturbed whilst basking, they rapidly fly off with zig-zag movements, only to land a few metres away and continue sunbathing. After mating, females carefully select coarse grass blades for egg-laying, suitably exposed, in places such as eroded trackways or bridlepaths where hoofs have made an impression. Exposed rootlets on tracks are sometimes used by the summer-brood butterflies for depositing eggs. The egg-laying site will be one which receives periodic sunshine and protection from persistent winds.

Distribution: Apart from high mountainous country, the Wall Brown is common in England, Wales and Ireland, but only reaches south-west Scotland. It is most frequently found there along the Cumbrian coastline.

MOUNTAIN RINGLET
Erebia epiphron

Wingspan: 35 mm (♂), 38 mm (♀)　　　　　**Status:** R

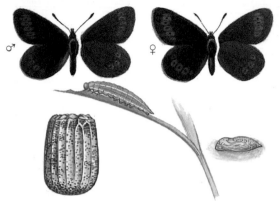

Typical habitat: Upland, boggy grassland grazed by sheep

On the wing: Mid-June – July

Adult: The bodies of both adults are extremely hairy and these hairs extend on to the upper surface of the dark-brown wings, near the body. All four wings show a marginal band of orange patches with central black dots, which are frequently larger in the female. She also has more distinct orange markings, but apart from size, both sexes are similar in appearance. The number of patches on each wing is extremely variable. Underside wing markings are similar to the upper surface, but the pigments are fainter and the dots and patches may be fewer.

Life cycle: The butterfly is single brooded, with pale-yellow, orange-blotched and vertically-ridged eggs laid on the low stems of mat grass. They hatch within eighteen days. The caterpillars are nocturnal feeders at first, feeding at the tips of the foodplant. When full-grown, they are green with white stripes and have two ochre-coloured tail points. They hibernate from late August until mid-March. The larval stage lasts nearly ten months before the caterpillar spins a loose cocoon low down in the grass and changes into the chrysalis. This is pale green, with fine brown stripes, and hatches after twenty-one days.

Observation and behaviour: Mountain Ringlets live in isolated colonies at high altitude, where their only wild foodplant, mat grass, is loosely grazed by red deer and sheep. They are sedentary and colonies remain in the same area each year. Although sunshine makes them active, only the males may be regularly seen, with their low-level, weak and indecisive flight, visiting thyme and tormentil for nectar and then basking with open wings. The females are less restless and prefer to roost deep in the vegetation, unless egg-laying.

Distribution: Distribution is restricted to Scotland and the central Lake District, where the colonies are very localized. There are many areas with suitable larval foodplant, but without butterflies. Although colonies in the Lake District are found below 200 metres, most occur between 500 to 800 metres. In Scotland sea-level populations occur, but the majority are true mountain-dwellers, breeding at between 450 and 800 metres. The best sites contain thousands of individuals: in Scotland, the Grampians around Glen Clova and east to Ben Nevis, and in Inverness, around Newtonmore.

SCOTCH ARGUS
Erebia aethiops

Wingspan: 35 mm (♂), 40 mm (♀)

Status: R

Typical habitat: Damp moorland, rough grassy hillsides
On the wing: July – August
Adult: The upperwings are dark brown with rust-red patches on all four wings. Patches on the hindwings are separate, but those on the forewings join to form an attractive band. All the patches are enhanced by black eyespots bearing white pupils. Generally only the silver-banded brown hindwing is revealed when the butterfly rests, when it resembles a dead leaf. The forewings are pulled downwards, so that the eyespots and orange markings on their undersides are concealed. Male coloration on the upper surface is darker than the female and overall, males are smaller. Those butterflies found in north-east Scotland tend to be smaller than populations elsewhere, with fewer spots and narrower wings.
Life cycle: The ridged and barrel-shaped egg is pale yellow, with pink speckles; despite being quite large, it is difficult to find. It is laid singly in August on leaves deep within clumps of purple or blue moor-grass (the latter

being the favourite foodplant in Cumbria). After fourteen days the egg hatches, with the caterpillar hiding in tussocks during the day, and feeding near the grass leaf-tips at night. Feeding continues until October, when the larva is full-grown and enters hibernation at the base of foodplant tussocks. It remains there until the following March. In the spring, feeding begins again. In total, the larval stage lasts around ten months, before the yellow-brown pupa is formed.

Observation and behaviour: The isolated colonies, sometimes numbering over 10,000 individuals, occur at altitudes ranging from sea level to around 500 metres, lower down the slopes than colonies of Mountain Ringlet. Damp grassy moor is the main habitat, especially in sheltered valleys where the grasses develop into tall, dense tussocks. The warm, south-facing margins of birch scrub or the rides in young conifer plantations, provide suitable alternative sites, as long as the sun reaches them. During sunny weather, males become active, patrolling low over the grass-heads looking for resting females, who spend most of their time feeding or basking. Males will drop down to ground level and inquisitively examine all dark objects, including leaves, in case they could be a potential mate. Apart from these reconnaissance flights, males generally spend their time roosting below the flower-heads of purple moor-grass, although they are active on overcast days when the air temperature is high. Both sexes obtain nectar from any available moorland flower, including heather.

Distribution: Despite local extinctions in the southern part of its range, the butterfly is numerous in its northern localities. At one time the Scotch Argus was found in Yorkshire and Northumberland, but its English distribution is now confined to the Lake District. The Inner Hebrides, Highlands and southern uplands remain the stronghold of this species. Here, variable races are found, differing in size and markings.

MARBLED WHITE
Melanargia galathea

Wingspan: 53 mm (♂), 58 mm (♀)   **Status:** R

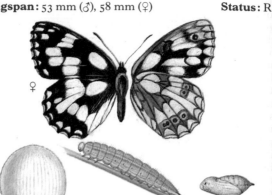

Typical habitat: Long mixed grassland, clifftops, railway embankments, verges, young plantation rides and chalk and limestone hillsides

On the wing: Late June – August in a single brood

Adult: Because of the beautiful black-and-white reticulated wing- markings, the Marbled White cannot be confused with any other butterfly. Both sexes have a characteristic slow, flapping flight, during which the markings can be easily distinguished. The females are larger, with paler markings than the male. Underside wing patterns are paler than upperside, and tend to be more olive in the female.

Life cycle: The round, white eggs are laid during July to mid-August and hatch after twenty days. They are impossible to find in the wild because the female alights on tall grasses, vibrates her abdomen and then takes off just as the egg is about to be laid, so that the egg drops into the vegetation and is lost from view. Immediately upon hatching, the pale-yellow caterpillar hibernates, concealed in tall grass, without feeding. In February feeding begins; a variety of grasses may be eaten, depending on the site, including red fescue, sheep's fescue, timothy, cock's-foot and tor grass. By June the brown or green larvae are full-grown, having fed on grass blades at night and hidden in the tussocks during the daytime. The off-white pupa is formed, unattached, at the bottom of grass tussocks. This stage lasts for around twenty-eight days, during May to July.

Observation and behaviour: On bright days whenever the sun shines and the temperature is above 15°C, this species is active, greedily feeding on nectar from knap-weed, thistles, scabious and bramble. Often, pairing takes place on these nectar-bearing flowers. The butterfly lives in discrete colonies, especially on chalk and limestone hillsides with the perfect balance of shelter and exposure to the sun. One field with mixed grasses and some shelter provided by scrub vegetation, may contain thousands of Marbled White butterflies, whereas a neighbouring field will be completely ignored.

On hazy days with a thin cover of cloud, the butterflies bask with their wings wide open, especially towards late afternoon. However, in full sunlight they close their wings, reducing the surface area exposed to the sun and therefore controlling body heat.

Distribution: Although the Marbled White is one of the most common European butterflies, its British range is extremely localized. Despite healthy colonies occurring on the South Downs, it is scarce in much of south-east England, becoming increasingly more widespread to-wards the south-west. Chalk grassland in Hampshire, Wiltshire, Dorset and Somerset is particularly well-inhabited but the species is very isolated on similar grassland on the North Downs. Although a few small colonies occur in south-west Yorkshire and Lincolnshire, the populations are declining because of habitat destruc-tion from ploughing and agricultural developments. Loss of habitat throughout the butterfly's range is causing the decline of many established colonies.

GRAYLING
Hipparchia semele

Wingspan: 55 mm (♂), 60 mm (♀)   **Status:** R

Typical habitat: Heaths, sand dunes and grassy cliffs, also dry hillsides with bare patches of soil

On the wing: July – September in a single brood

Adult: Both sexes of the Grayling are similar, with the female being larger and paler. The pale-brown upper wing-surface is rarely seen because this butterfly always perches with closed wings. Only the hindwings are then visible, revealing a pale-grey ground colour, marked with brown and dark-grey patches. The darker markings are nearer to the body, bordered by a characteristic zig-zag line running across the middle of each hindwing. These markings totally camouflage the Grayling when it rests on grey-brown sand. Occasionally, the forewings are flicked out, revealing a brown-orange patch on their underside, with two distinguishable black eyespots bearing white pupils. Around the margins of each forewing runs a light-grey border flecked with brown.

Life cycle: The eggs, which are numerously ridged,

white, and nearly spherical, are laid individually on a variety of grasses, or on other unlikely vegetation such as twigs. After eighteen days, a pale-cream caterpillar emerges, and feeds nocturnally on the blades of grass, concealing itself at the base of the tussock during the day. The best way to find the caterpillar is with a torch during nights in late May and June, when it is fully grown. After a second moult it hibernates, low down in the herbage, and remains concealed until the spring, when it resumes feeding. The larval stage lasts between nine and ten months. From late June into August, the red-brown pupa is formed just below the ground surface, making its location impossible without careful digging.

Observation and behaviour: The butterfly is abundant throughout the British Isles on well-drained soil and doesn't discriminate between alkaline, chalk or acidic sandstone. Grayling breeding on limestone soils are whiter on the hindwing underside than those breeding on acidic soils. The species always prefers those sites where the soil layer is thin and loose rocks and rubble lie strewn on the surface. Grass cover may be sparse; sand dunes and eroding cliff faces are popular haunts in which hundreds of butterflies may form a colony.

Although they can fly strongly, Grayling like to fly and bask alternately. They perch on warm, dry, patches of bare ground and close their wings, then tilt the leading edge of their wings towards the sun, so that no shadow is cast. Even at close range, the butterfly seems to disappear. Once disturbed, both sexes will take off rapidly, before gliding down to another warm ground patch a few metres away. Courtship also occurs on the ground, with the male landing in front of the female and rapidly quivering his wings.

Distribution: Many formerly good heathland sites have been destroyed by agricultural development and the Grayling has become decidedly more coastal. Throughout southern and western England, the Grayling is locally common and it also breeds on the Hebrides and Western Isles.

GATEKEEPER, OR HEDGE BROWN
Pyronia tithonus
Wingspan: 40 mm (♂), 47 mm (♀)   **Status:** R

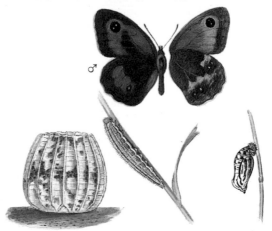

Typical habitat: Hedgerows, country lanes, woodland rides and scrubland

On the wing: July – September

Adult: The sexes are similar, with golden-brown upperwings and darker brown margins. However, males are smaller and brighter than females, with a distinctive dark patch of scent scales in the middle of the forewing, as illustrated. Black eye spots near the apex of the forewings in both sexes, characteristically contain two white pupils, compared to the single pupil of similar species. The undersides are duller, with subdued orange on the forewing and brown on the hindwing.

Life cycle: From mid-July until September, the spherical, ridged eggs are laid singly on various grasses or low herbage in partial shade. Within twenty days they hatch and the small, cream caterpillars feed on couch grass and red fescue before hibernating during the second or third instar. They are full-grown by the following May, and must be found by torchlight since they are nocturnal feeders, hiding by day at the base of the grass tussock. Two colour forms exist, the green and the brown, with the brown being the rarer of the two. The cream and brown-spotted chrysalis is difficult to find; it is suspended from grass and other vegetation before hatching after twenty-one days.

Observation and behaviour: This butterfly does not favour open grass downland, but is found wherever hedges and scrub vegetation provide shelter. Since it likes to feed on rich supplies of nectar, it is never far from bramble, in which it also roosts at night, field scabious, marjoram, fleabane or common ragwort. Often groups of adults feed together whenever the sun is out; this is particularly noticeable during the peak emergence in August. Several thousand butterflies form the large, isolated colonies, which are never far from woodland. Even glades and rides a few metres wide can support breeding colonies. Although it rarely settles on the ground, the Gatekeeper regularly flits from one flower to another, and its quick and irregular flight is best observed during this activity.

Distribution: As hedgerows have been removed, numbers of this butterfly have declined, especially in East Anglia. It is still common in southern England and parts of south Wales, however, wherever shrubs and grasses grow close together. In recent years, populations have even increased in parts of the Thames Valley and Yorkshire. Generally speaking, the Gatekeeper may be regularly seen during late summer in the south. North of the Midlands, the butterfly population declines and Cumbria represents its northern limit. In Ireland it is only found on the southern coasts and around Dublin.

MEADOW BROWN
Maniola jurtina

Wingspan: 50 mm (♂), 55 mm (♀)   **Status:** R

♀

Typical habitat: Any grassy area, including hillsides, roadside verges and woodland rides

On the wing: Mid June – late September or early October

Adult: Because the sexes of the Meadow Brown are so different, they were once thought to be separate species. The female (*illustrated*) is larger than the male and so are the orange patches with black eyespots on her upper forewings. The rest of the upper wing-surface of the female is sandy brown, whereas that of the male is dark brown. At rest, the wings are generally closed and only the grey-orange hindwings are visible, with a characteristic zig-zag marking dividing them into two halves. Frequently, the Meadow Brown plays host to small red parasites, seen attached to the thorax near the wings.

Life cycle: The small, round, orange-blotched eggs are laid individually on to grass blades or dropped into loose vegetation near grass tussocks, while the female is perched. The favoured egg-laying site is grassland with both short and long turf species, because the small larvae prefer fine grasses such as smooth meadow grass, whereas the older caterpillars will eat cock's-foot grass, tor grass and slender false brome. During winter, the caterpillars partially hibernate low down in the herbage, but in spring they feed nocturnally on the grass blades and their green bodies covered in white hairs are easily found by torchlight. They fall to the ground and curl up whenever touched, and are then difficult to relocate. The green and black-striped pupa forms low down among the grasses, suspended from grass stems or blades, and within eighteen days the butterfly emerges.

Observation and behaviour: This species is sedentary and reluctant to try out its fluttering, weak flight until almost stepped upon. When the air temperatures rise above 13°C the Meadow Brown will fly above the grass, even on overcast days, sometimes late into the evening. It then roosts in long grass or on tall, meadow flower-heads. Large colonies exist wherever the grass is tall and lush with some shelter from scrub vegetation, but the butterfly is rarer wherever the turf is short and declines if grazing is prolonged. When the sunlight is diffused through thin cloud cover, Meadow Browns bask with open wings, but on totally overcast days or in full sunshine, hold their wings closed. Flower-heads of marjoram, field scabious, common knapweed and bramble will afford good views of this butterfly, which cannot resist a rich supply of nectar throughout the season.

Distribution: Although not often seen in town gardens, the Meadow Brown is arguably the most common species in the British Isles. However, within the last fifteen years it has disappeared from many of its original lowland sites, because these have been lost to agricultural developments. Open grassland below 200 metres still remains populated throughout the country, although the butterfly is not found on the Shetlands and is localized in Scotland.

SMALL HEATH
Coenonympha pamphilus

Wingspan: 34 mm (♂), 38 mm (♀)

Status: R

Typical habitat: Most grassy areas, including meadows, hillsides and pathways

On the wing: May – September in a succession of broods

Adult: Only the undersides of this butterfly are seen, because it always rests with wings tightly closed. The hindwing underside is grey-brown and darker near the body, with indistinct white dots near the margin. In fine weather the forewing is protruded from between the hindwings, revealing a bright orange patch with a black eyespot and single white pupil, near the apex.

Life cycle: Watching female Small Heaths egg-laying reveals that they are highly selective in their choice of site. Usually the yellow-green, indented eggs are laid singly on a variety of fine-bladed grasses and are difficult to find. Within fifteen days the caterpillars hatch, feeding at night but remaining low in the tussock during the daytime to avoid being hunted. Caterpillars can be found at all months of the year, because they overwinter in this stage, feeding whenever the weather is mild and probably during the day in this season. The pupae are equally difficult to locate, suspended from grass stems. They are attractive, with brown stripes contrasting against an overall light-green colour.

Observation and behaviour: Usually the Small Heath is a sedentary butterfly, but on warm days it is able to disperse to new sites on which grasses of various heights and species are growing. Not enough is known about ideal turf conditions for this species, but the best sites seem to be those on well-drained soils, where grasses of medium height offer sparse ground cover. Annual and woodland meadow grass and meadow fescue seem to be favourite larval grasses, but wherever finer grasses survive, so does the butterfly. Large populations occur on coastal sites, especially dunes and heaths, but old chalk downlands are equally popular with this species. The number of generations varies geographically and with the season, but the first is from May to July and the second is from July to August, with a partial brood in September flying as late as early October in favourable years. At night the butterfly roosts on flowers or old seed-heads and during the day feeds on wild thyme, buttercups, hawkweeds and marjoram, rapidly moving from one plant to another in undulating flight.

Distribution: The distribution of the Small Heath has remained unchanged over the last century, although as a result of habitat destruction, its populations have fallen. It is still one of the most common species throughout Britain, colonizing offshore islands and moorland over 700 metres, together with well-drained lowlands, hedgerows and road verges.

LARGE HEATH
Coenonympha tullia

Wingspan: 41 mm (♂ and ♀)   **Status:** R

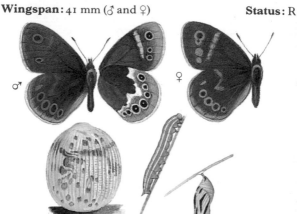

Typical habitat: Wet hillsides, peat bogs and moorland up to 800 metres

On the wing: Mid-June – July in a single brood

Adult: Apart from the fact that the female is slightly lighter, both sexes are similar, although this is one of our most variably-marked butterflies. Three distinct forms of Large Heath are found throughout its British distribution, which vary in size, base colour and eye-spot markings. In addition, butterflies of the same form can be dissimilar within any one colony, further confusing the observer. Since the butterfly always basks with wings closed, only the grey-brown undersides are seen. They vary as follows:

1 *Form davus* (*illustrated*) This is the most common form in southern Britain, extending to Shropshire, Cheshire and Staffordshire. The undersides are dark grey, with distinct, large eyespots on both wings. These spots are most attractive. Usually there are six or seven on the

hindwing and up to four on the forewing, black with white pupils and pale-yellow outer rings.

2 *Form polydama* Colonizing the Central Scottish Lowlands, Cumbria and north Yorkshire, this form is larger than *davus*, with paler wings. There is more brown on the forewing, and the eyespots are smaller and sometimes lack pupils.

3 *Form scotica* This form is the exception to the rule, because it often lacks eyespots completely and if they are present, they are extremely indistinct. *Scotica* is the largest form and also the most northern, colonizing the Outer Hebrides, Orkney and Shetland Islands as well as the Scottish Highlands. All markings are pale on wings with tawny uppersides and grey undersides.

Life cycle: The large, rounded egg with a flat top and numerous ridges is laid singly on the blades of white-beaked sedge, purple moor-grass or cotton grass, during July. Within a fortnight it hatches. The straw-coloured larva changes to green after its first skin moult. Around September, after the second moult, the larva hibernates, resuming feeding the following March. The caterpillar feeds at night, but as it grows, daytime feeding also takes place, with the larva chewing from the tip of the grass, downwards. Altogether the larval stage lasts about ten months. When fully grown, it is green with white stripes, and an unusually large head on a long, tapering body. The green chrysalis is difficult to find, hanging from a pad of silk in dense undergrowth. It resembles that of a Small Heath, with brown stripes on the wing cases.

Observation and behaviour: As it has such a short flight time, it is necessary to plan observation of this butterfly well in advance. The boggy hillsides and upland moors colonized by the Large Heath are also frequently partly under water and therefore dangerous for the observer. Isolated colonies will often contain several thousand adults.

Distribution: This species is restricted to Scotland, mid and northern Wales, northern England and throughout Ireland. In all these areas it is a rarity.

RINGLET
Aphantopus hyperantus

Wingspan: 48 mm (♂), 52 mm (♀)   **Status:** R

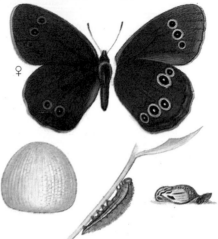

Typical habitat: Woodland rides and glades, sheltered hedgerows and shaded verges

On the wing: Mid-June – August in a single brood

Adult: Both sexes of the Ringlet are a uniform brown, which is particularly dark in the male, giving the appearance of almost black upperwings. The outer margin of all the wings is defined by a white fringe and eyespots appear on both surfaces.

Life cycle: The butterflies mate on bramble flower-heads or in long grass, but the conical eggs are dropped at random into tall grasses while the female is flying, and are impossible to find. For this reason, little is known about the range of larval foodplants. Upon hatching in July or August, the small caterpillars crawl to the grasses on which they feed; cock's-foot grass, annual meadow grass, wood false brome and tufted hair grass are some of their known favourites. Whilst quite small, the larvae hibernate. They resume feeding the following spring, reaching full size by June. They are nocturnal feeders, hiding low in the grass tussocks by day, and as dusk arrives, crawling to the top of the grass blades and feeding from the tip downwards. Searching damp grassland at night with a torch, where the turf is about thirty centimetres high, is the best way to find the caterpillars. They will curl up and drop to the ground if disturbed. The pupa is formed within a scanty silken cocoon, low down in grass tussocks, and is difficult to find. It hatches within fourteen days.

Observation and behaviour: Although the Ringlet is active when the temperature is above 14°C, it is one of the few butterflies which flies during dull, showery weather. It will also fly late into the evening, after sunset, especially if disturbed from its grass-stem roosts. Its flight is weak and fluttering, generally low over the grass-heads, and the butterfly is rarely seen flying on windy days. By nature, Ringlets are restless, taking numerous nectar-seeking flights to bramble, privet, common knapweed and marjoram. Because they frequently flap about and crawl into bramble thickets, their wings quickly become very tattered. At rest, they sit with wings tightly closed, exposing the characteristic group of yellow-ringed, black eyespots. These markings are often pecked at by birds, thus diverting attention from the vulnerable head, and leaving the butterfly with functional, but holed, wings. Ringlets are sedentary butterflies, forming large colonies of many thousands wherever the ground is damp (though not under water), and grasses grow sheltered from wind and in the shade, usually on the cooler, north-facing slopes and hollows of scrub grassland.

Distribution: Found throughout much of England, Wales, central Scotland and Ireland, this is one of our most widespread butterflies. Industrial pollution has affected its distribution, however, and it is largely absent from the Midlands, London, south Wales and south-east Scotland. Since the species dislikes dry conditions, it declined after the drought of 1976.

MONARCH, OR MILKWEED
Danaus plexippus

Wingspan: 76 – 114 mm (♂ and ♀)   **Status:** RM

The butterfly is shown three-quarters
of its actual size

Typical habitat: Parks and gardens, wherever flowers abound

On the wing: July – September

Adult: The upper side of the wings are chestnut-brown, with distinctive black veins and broad black margins containing two parallel rows of white spots. The apical area of the forewings has larger white spots. The male is distinguished by a dark patch of black scent scales, attached to a vein in the centre of the hindwings; the wing undersides are similarly marked. The body is black with white markings, particularly on the head and thorax, and the antennae are completely black.

Life cycle: Since the larval foodplant, milkweed, is not indigenous to Britain, the butterfly is unable to breed here. The pale-green, acorn-shaped eggs are laid individually on the underside of the leaves. After three days the caterpillar emerges, eats the discarded shell and grows rapidly for sixteen days, reaching a maximum size of fifty-six millimetres. Its head is yellow with black bands and the rest of the body is lemon-yellow with black-and-white hoops down its length. Towards the front and rear ends of the body, a pair of black tentacles can be clearly seen, which are longer at the head end.

Observation and behaviour: Since the nineteenth century, Monarchs have bred on the Canary Islands and some of the British sightings have originated from there. It is common in North America, where it is famous for its mass migrations each spring and autumn. Some American immigrants are blown towards Britain as westerly gales disperse them out towards the sea. The butterfly first appeared here in 1876, but more recent sightings include those of 1968, when over sixty individuals were seen in the south and again in 1981, when 140 butterflies were reported in the West Country.

Distribution: Since breeding this species in captivity has become popular, it is difficult to distinguish sightings of genuine immigrants from those of escapees from butterfly farms and private collectors. True migrants occur in the Scillies, Ireland, the West Country and Sussex.

RECOMMENDED SOCIETIES
TO JOIN

1 British Butterfly Conservation Society, Tudor House, Quorn, Nr. Loughborough, Leicestershire, LE12 8AD

Anyone interested in the future of butterflies in Britain should join the British Butterfly Conservation Society, the premier organization concerned with the study and conservation of butterflies. There are regional branches and all members receive an informative quarterly bulletin.

2 Amateur Entomologists' Society, 355 Hounslow Road, Hanworth, Middlesex

With an active membership, this society caters for amateurs keen to study all forms of insect life, including beetles and dragonflies as well as butterflies.

3 Royal Society of Nature Conservation, The Green, Nettleham, Lincolnshire, LN2 2NR

This society pioneered nature conservation in Britain, and instigated Government support of it. The forty-eight County Naturalists' Trusts are co-ordinated by the RSNC, and protect wildlife at a local level by purchasing nature reserves, many of which are homes for butterflies.

4 Institute of Terrestrial Ecology (ITE), Monks Wood Experimental Station, Abbots Ripton, Huntingdon, PE17 2LS

This is a professional investigative unit, part of the Natural Environment Research Council, performing a wide range of biological research. The Biological Records Centre (BRC) is part of the ITE and is responsible for the National Biological Data Bank on all plant and animal distributions. A national butterfly-monitoring scheme was run by the ITE from 1967 to 1981, using observations sent to the Institute by 2,000 amateur contributors. The results were compiled and collated, and the butterfly distribution information in this book is largely based on them, together with information gathered by the National Butterfly Recording Scheme, which began in 1983.

BUTTERFLY FARMS

Worldwide Butterflies, Compton House, Sherborne, Dorset, DT9 4QN

The London Butterfly House, Syon Park, Brentford, Middlesex, TW7 5N

The Living World, Seven Sisters Country Park, Exceat, Seaford, East Sussex, BN25 4AD

Blenheim Butterfly Centre, Blenheim Palace, Woodstock, Oxford OX7 1PX

New Forest Butterfly Farm, Longdown, Ashurst, Nr. Southampton, SO4 4UH

Le Friquet Butterfly Centre, Le Friquet, Castel, Guernsey, Channel Islands

Haute Tombette Butterfly House, St. Mary, Jersey, Channel Islands

I.O.W. Butterfly World, Medina Garden Centre, Staplers Road, Wootton, Ryde, Isle of Wight

The Butterfly Centre (Eastbourne) Ltd., Royal Parade, Eastbourne, Sussex, BN22 7HQ

Padstow Bird Gardens (Butterfly House), Padstow, Cornwall, PL28 8BB

Solva Nectarium Ltd., The Old Chapel, Lower Solva, Nr. Haverfordwest, Dyfed, West Wales.

Hazlehead Zoo (Butterfly House), Aberdeen Leisure Centre, Hazlehead Park, Hazlehead Avenue, Aberdeen.

Loose Valley Butterfly Farm, Old Loose Hill, Loose, Maidstone, Kent

Butterfly World, Wealden Woodlands, Herne Common, Nr. Canterbury, Kent

Butterfly Safari, Burnham Road, South Woodham Ferrers, Essex

Stratford Butterfly Farm, Tramway Walk, Swan's Nest Lane, Stratford-upon-Avon, Warwickshire, CV37 7LS

Edinburgh Butterfly Farm, Melville Nurseries, Lasswade, Nr. Edinburgh, Midlothian, EH18 1AZ

Weymouth Butterfly Farm, Lodmoor Country Park, Greenhill, Weymouth, Dorset, 2D4 7SX

The Butterfliarium, Jackamoors, Theobalds Park Road, Crews Hill, Enfield, Middlesex

Butterfly World, Yockleton, Shrewsbury, SY5 9PU

Weston Park Butterfly Farm, Weston Park, Weston-under-Lizard, Nr. Shifnal, Shropshire, TF11 8LE

Great Yarmouth Butterfly Centre, Marine Parade, Great Yarmouth, Norfolk, NR30 3AH

Pili Pilas, Ffordd Penmyndd, Porthaethwy, Ynys Mon, Gwyndd, Wales

Butterfly Exhibition, High Street, Bourton-on-the-Water, Gloucestershire

Flutters, Pinfold Lane, Bridlington, East Yorks, YO16 5XP

Buckfast Butterfly Farm, Buckfastleigh Steam and Leisure Park, East Buckfastleigh, Devon

English Country Gardens, Charlecote Nurseries, Charlecote, Warwick, CV35 9ER

Cheddar Tropical House, Cheddar Gorge, Somerset

Butterfly Centre, MacFarlane's Garden and Leisure Centre, Swingfield, nr. Dover, Kent

Windmill Garden Centre and Butterfly Farm, Mill Lane, Herne, Kent

Butterfly World, Hornsea Pottery, Hornsea, Yorks, HU18 1UD

Longleat Garden Centre, Longleat, Warminster, Wiltshire

Newent Butterfly Centre, Spring Bank, Birches Lane, Newent, Gloucestershire

Drum Manor Butterfly Garden, County Tyrone, Northern Ireland

Butterfly Jungle, Royal Floral Hall, East Parade, Rhyl, North Wales

Mole Hall Wildlife Park, Widdington, Saffron Walden, Essex

Longstone Centre, St Mary's, Isle of Scilly, Cornwall, TR21 0NW

Trent Valley Garden Centre, Doncaster Road, Scunthorpe, Lincolnshire

Solent Butterfly House, Hammonds Garden Centre, Stubbington, Hants, PO14 2NF

NURSERIES AND WILD-FLOWER
SEED MERCHANTS

Butterflies generally lay their eggs on wild flowers, and also obtain nectar from them. Wild flowers can easily be introduced into your garden by purchasing seeds or plants from the following specialists:

Chiltern Seeds, Bortree Stile, Ulverston, Cumbria

Careby Manor Gardens, Careby, Stamford, Lincolnshire

John Chambers, 15 Westleigh Road, Barton Seagrave, Kettering, Northamptonshire

Emorsgate Seeds, Terrington Court, Terrington St. Clement, Norfolk

Mr Fothergill's Seeds, Gazeley Road, Kentford, Newmarket, Suffolk, CB8 7QB

Kingsfield Tree Nursery, Broadenham Lane, Winsham, Chard, Somerset

Naturescape, Little Orchard, Whatton-in-the-Vale, Nottinghamshire, NG13 9EP

The Seed Bank and Exchange, Cowcombe Farm, Gypsy Lane, Chalford, Stroud, Gloucester, GL6 8HP

Suffolk Herbs, Sawyers Farm, Little Cornard, Sudbury, Suffolk, CO10 ONY

Sutton Seeds, S. Dobie and Son and Carters Tested Seeds, Hele Road, Torquay, Devon, TQ2 7QJ

Thomson and Morgan, London Road, Ipswich, Suffolk, IP2 0BA

Unwins Seeds, Histon, Cambridge, CB4 4LE

RECOMMENDED BOOKS

Brooks, M. and Knight, C. *A Complete Guide to British Butterflies*, Jonathan Cape, London, 1982

A photographic guide to the life cycle of every species

Feltwell, Dr. J. (principal author) *Butterflies*, Reader's Digest and National Trust, London, 1984

A well-illustrated guide in the Nature Notebooks Series, with concise notes and an excellent butterfly-site gazetteer

Gibbons, R. and Wilson, P. *The Wildlife Photographer – A Complete Guide*, Blandford Press, Dorset, 1986

An extensively illustrated, highly readable book on all aspects of nature photography, including that of insects, with full explanations of techniques and equipment used

Howarth, T.G. *Colour Identification Guide to Butterflies of the British Isles*, Viking, London, 1984

Useful text on butterfly classification, life history, structure and distribution, with stunning and accurate colour plates, many copied from the originals of F.W. Frohawk

Oates, M. *Garden Plants for Butterflies*, Masterton, 1985

A useful pocket guide to species found in the garden, together with full details on how to encourage butterflies into your own back yard

Thomas, Dr J.A. *RSNC Guide to Butterflies of the British Isles*, Country Life Books, Middlesex, 1986

Probably one of the most thorough and topical guides to British butterflies, with over seventy colour photographs

INDEX TO SPECIES

Page numbers in heavy type indicate the butterfly's main description